UNFOLDING THE ECO-WAVE

Unfolding the Eco-wave

Why Renewal is Pivotal

A. V. RYZHENKOV

JOHN WILEY & SONS, LTD
Chichester • New York • Weinheim • Brisbane • Singapore • Toronto

Copyright © 2000 by John Wiley & Sons Ltd,
Baffins Lane, Chichester,
West Sussex PO19 1UD, England

National   01243 779777
International (+44) 1243 779777
e-mail(for orders and customer service enquiries): cs-books@wiley.co.uk
Visit our Home Page on http://www.wiley.co.uk
or http://www.wiley.com

Other Wiley Editorial Offices

John Wiley & Sons, Inc., 605 Third Avenue,
New York, NY 10158-0012, USA

WILEY-VCH Verlag GmbH, Pappelallee 3,
D-69469 Weinheim, Germany

Jacaranda Wiley Ltd, 33 Park Road, Milton,
Queensland 4064, Australia

John Wiley & Sons (Asia) Pte Ltd, 2 Clementi Loop #02-01,
Jin Xing Distripark, Singapore 129809

John Wiley & Sons (Canada) Ltd, 22 Worcester Road,
Rexdale, Ontario M9W 1L1, Canada

Library of Congress Cataloging-in-Publication Data

Ryzhenkov, A. V. (Aleksandr Vladimirovich)
    Unfolding the eco-wave : why renewal is pivotal / A. V. Ryzhenkov.
        p.   cm.
    Includes bibliographical references and index.
    ISBN 0-471-60792-4 (alk. paper)
    1. Capitalism. 2. Environmental economics. 3. Economics,
Mathematical. 4. Economics — Research. I. Title.
HB501.R96   1999
333.7 — dc21   99–37218
                                                              CIP

British Library Cataloguing in Publication Data

A catalogue record for this book is available from the British Library

ISBN 0-471-60792-4

Typeset in 10/12pt Times by Laser Words, Madras, India
Printed and bound in Great Britain by Bookcraft (Bath) Ltd, Midsomer Norton, Somerset.
This book is printed on acid-free paper responsibly manufactured from sustainable forestry, in which at least two trees are planted for each one used for paper production.

To my parents

CONTENTS

ACKNOWLEDGEMENTS

The British painter Thomas Gainsborough is reported to have said that portraits were his profession but landscape painting was his pleasure. Similarly, mathematical economics is my profession but gaming and computer simulations are my pleasure.

The present book is based on scientific research over a number of years. Parts of the research were carried out at the State University and Institute of Economics and Industrial Engineering in Novosibirsk, the Austrian Institute for Economic Research in Vienna, German universities in Mannheim, Hamburg and Bremen, and the Worcester Polytechnic Institute (WPI) in the USA. Earlier results were used in lectures at the Novosibirsk State University, presented at several international conferences and published elsewhere.

Professor Yu. L. Ershov, Professor S. V. Kazantsev, Professor V. V. Kuleshov, Dr V. E. Seliverstov, Professor K. K. Valtukh, Professor V. N. Vragov and my other colleagues in Russia facilitated the scientific work in Novosibirsk. My Austrian colleagues F. Butschek, H. Kramer, S. Schleicher and G. Thury gave me a unique opportunity to learn econometrics and apply it to real statistical data.

An intellectual influence by Professor K. K. Valtukh will be clearly obvious in the following pages. Professor R. M. Goodwin's encouraging letters have lent wings to this research endeavour. A particular debt of gratitude is owed to Professor Peter Milling, especially for his skilful treatment of system dynamics in lectures that I attended at Mannheim University.

Through the efforts of Dr C. Tiby, Dr J. Schmidt-Tophoff and other associates of Arthur D. Little International in Wiesbaden I acquired valuable experience of being a freelancer in industrial consulting. I am very grateful to Professor K. Wohlmuth for his support of my research on Russia's technology policy, partially reflected in this book.

Professor B. Martensson (Bremen University) helped me to simulate long waves with his valuable program *Gnans*. Professor M. Myrtveit (ModellData AS in Norway) and Professor L. Vavik (Stord/Haugesund College, Norway) provided me with the *Powersim* learning environment. The valuable research assistance of Dr Irina Jäger was also appreciated.

The exciting flight simulator and papers on long waves by Professor John Sterman awoke my latent interest in the field of system dynamics more than 10 years ago. The comments of Professor Kh. Saeed, Professor M. Radzicki and other American colleagues have been invaluable. I have enjoyed their hospitality during the final stages of this work.

It would never have been finished without the ingenuity and supportive optimism of Dr J. Agbenyega, Publishing Editor for Finance at John Wiley & Sons, Ltd. A special appreciation is reserved for the anonymous referees of this eco-mathematical libretto. Philip R. Tye has provided very intelligent corrections to the final composition.

The Alexander von Humboldt Foundation provided financial support in Germany and donated the computer facilities for research at the home Institute. Funding by the World Society Foundation and the Avina Foundation has made possible my stay at the WPI.

The Russian writer Vladimir Nabokov thought that dream and reality merge in love. This book is a baby of the cultural cross-over and my love ... for system dynamics.

Pointers on *Powersim* and *Vensim* diagrams, these Cupid's arrows, are used to unveil the beauty of mathematical relationships; Father Time is seemingly rendered powerless by computer simulation runs of a deliberate duration, and even the Sun, Truth's emblem, is shining above my head at the time of writing. The reader will soon become aware of what earthly things lie subject beneath Truth's fair, voluptuous beauty.

These images arise from a picture *Time Unveiling Truth* by the Italian artist Giovanni Battista Tiepolo (1696–1770) in the Fine Arts Museum in Boston. In this picture, Cupid, whose quiver of arrows remains on the ground, is rendered powerless by Father Time. Oh boy, if you had had a computer model! Clever and eloquent comments on this masterpiece have influenced my vocabulary and imagination.

INTRODUCTION

One nation can and should learn from others. And even when a society has got upon the right track for the discovery of the natural laws of its movement — and it is the ultimate aim of this work, to lay bare the economic law of motion of modern society — it can neither clear by bold leaps, nor remove by legal enactments, the obstacles offered by successive phases of its normal development. But it can shorten and lessen the birth-pangs.

Karl Marx (1978a: 20)

A capitalist, profit-oriented economy has the inherent ability to initiate, diffuse and adjust to technical change. Unlike previous modes of production with their conservative technological base, industrial capitalism is characterised by evolutionary and revolutionary technological transformations based on a systematic and wide-scale usage of theoretical and applied knowledge (mostly natural sciences). On the one hand, technological progress disturbs market equilibrium, on the other, it exerts a stabilising influence on economic dynamics and income distribution.

Market prices transmit information (money talks). The incentives and threats of a capitalist economy transmitted by market prices during the dynamic process of competition lead to the discovery and dissemination of new knowledge.

Among the critical subsystems of society, as a living system, there are associator (education, R&D, etc.) and memory (data banks, scientific information service, libraries, museums, etc.) which enable accumulation of knowledge in socially concentrated and integrated forms in spite of the dispersal of individually possessed knowledge (see Miller 1978: 766–768). These information-processing subsystems are used by government, entrepreneurs and other economic agents on an increasing scale.

It is known from economic theory that market forces do not necessarily lead to optimal investment decisions because present prices do not reflect the cost and demand conditions that will exist in the future. A reliance on the market alone cannot lead to socially satisfactory results; in particular, evident underinvestment in R&D and the environment is typical of a capitalist economy if market incentives are not supplemented by public policies and regulations.

It has been recognised that the world is an open dissipative system. The economic growth experienced world-wide has been inherently driving the world economy to a scale, that is, a level of throughput, which may exceed the environment's carrying capacity. It cannot withstand a systematic increase of the throughput of matter-energy, but it can support exponential increases of information and knowledge: "sustainability and development might be compatible if you could create value and satisfy people's needs by increasing the information component of what's produced and diminishing the amount of stuff" (Magretta 1997: 82).[1]

For a human being, learning is a change of behaviour via a change of consciousness. Learning occurs in all social forms, yet it is conceived in the emerging information societies as the very base for functioning and evolution. According to general living systems theory, the evolution of societies depends primarily upon accumulation and transmission of learned information. These information processes mean not only acquisition of knowledge but the power of organisation as well. Despite the overall trend, evolution does not in every case progress in the direction of greater complexity, adaptability, self-regulation and social integration. In fact, collective learning processes can also proceed in pathological forms (see Miller 1978).

It is widely acknowledged that the central problems with which Marx wrestled are still with us. His methodological achievements, however, have not been assimilated by some modern streams of economic thought. This book consciously applies elements of Marx's dialectical logic and his deep insights into capital accumulation. It also tries to absorb the ingenuity of different theoretical schools of economic thought.

My *central hypothesis* is that the developed capitalist countries are preparing to enter a new phase of development, which has been termed *eco-capitalism* by forerunners. This transition is likely to occur within the next (fifth) Kondratiev cycle, or *eco-wave*, after prior fulfilment of essential prerequisites. This book looks forward and back, unveiling and explaining the emerging eco-wave in step-by-step manner. An integrative system dynamics methodology thereby serves as the Ariadne thread.

The reader will see a difference between this approach and that of the ragged man in the Elihu Vedder picture *The Questioner of the Sphinx* (1863).[2] This character huddles fearfully at the statue's mouth, seeking answers to the mysteries of life. We challenge the artist's idea of hopelessness of human beings before immutable natural laws.

Chapter 1 touches the fundamental theoretical issue of the relationships between prices and labour values. Marx's economic theory predicts that the price of commodities depends, *ceteris paribus*, on the productivity of labour, and this variable depends, in turn, on the scale of production.

Estimations of the pace of technological progress are based on growth rates of labour productivity. The theoretical price model is tested against Austrian data for 1975–84: it helps to reveal and explain the close association between changes in productivity and relative prices. Fabricant's and Verdoorn's empirical laws are statistically tested and justified for this period. Uncovering increasing returns helps to show the limitations of the orthodox neo-classical theory of value and income distribution. The theory of value is connected with the concept of economic growth, fluctuations and control in the following chapters.

Chapter 2 displays simulation experiments with a disequilibrium model of capitalist reproduction developed at Novosibirsk University by K. K. Valtukh with assistance from F. E. Pusep. The first experiment displays regularities of reproduction on a decreasing scale traditionally rarely treated in economic textbooks. It is indispensable for a treatment of Russia's downward spiral in Chapter 6.

The second and third experiments demonstrate how production could be extended. These case studies show that the applied theoretical framework can lead to propositions deduced or derived empirically in industrial economics. This part of the book focuses on an inherent interplay between diffusion of innovations and the evolving competitive environment. It considers capital mobility, firm entries and exits, movements in prices and quantities, disequilibrium in production and trade.

It is shown that economic agents appear to obey the objective law of value through decentralised decision-making in accordance with prices, quantities and profitability signals. Private commodity producers do not fully use the potential of the economy, but learning improves the outcomes of their activity. The importance of imitation for economic growth is emphasised.

These laboratory experiments illustrate the irreversibility of economic development and show a tendency towards a higher level of self-organisation judging by some indicators of efficiency and effectiveness. Additional information from outside (for example, teaching) accelerates the progressive evolution of the modelling system.

Participants in gaming experiments not only reveal information embodied in the initial conditions and rules of the game (memory), but also create/store new (synergetic) information via decision-making. In particular, they keep in mind the choices of techniques and give preference to the definite connections between different technologies among a broader set of possibilities. In addition, collective learning and teaching provide a new semantic level of information and higher economic efficiency. The key organisational feature of the economy in the information age, namely the complementary nature of competition, co-operation and co-ordination, becomes notably visual.

It is well known that Karl Marx left unsolved a number of theoretical problems, including the issue of reduction of a qualified labour to a simple labour in his theory of commodity and surplus value. The Valtukh information value hypothesis is an attempt to generalise the labour theory of value and free it from internal contradictions. This hypothesis plays an important role in modelling capitalist reproduction on an increasing scale in the following chapters of this book.

"The current wildfire revival of interest in growth theory" and the need for greater practical relevance of this theory make it necessary to reconsider the orthodox propositions in economics (Solow 1994). The entrenchment of the latter in standard textbooks may partially explain the rather slow progress of economics compared with physics and biology.

Specifically, two modern approaches to cyclical growth are compared in Chapters 3–5: the extended neo-classical and post-Marxian (for simplicity, the extended neo-classical model below is called the neo-classical model). They are trying to develop the pioneering work of R. M. Goodwin (1972) that defined a predator–prey model for the share of labour in national income and the employment ratio in a highly stylised capitalist economy. The latter generates a path of development where growth and cycles appear simultaneously without having distinct causes. The very notion of cyclical growth is a profound synthesis indeed.

In Goodwin's model with exogenous technical progress, income distribution is determined by the dynamics of real wages and productivity (Goodwin 1972). The interaction of income distribution with capital accumulation generates business cycles. The model, being written in continuous time, belongs to the class of models of the Lotka–Volterra type. The employment ratio serves as the prey, while the wage share acts as a predator. In order to obtain reasonable economic solutions, it is necessary to put some restrictions on the parameters.

Both approaches, neo-classical and post-Marxian, use a Kaldorian technical progress function to capture endogenous technical progress. The extended neo-classical model enriches the earlier Solow (1956) model by having endogenous technical progress (Kaldor 1957) and non-instantaneous clearing of the labour market (van der Ploeg 1983; Zhang 1988).

The post-Marxian Goodwin-like model of fluctuating growth retains these properties as well. It allows for the effects of composition of capital upon real wages, thus augmenting the key relationship — the real Phillips curve. This model typically yields the persistence of unemployment and is in agreement with Kaldor's stylised facts of economic growth (Ryzhenkov 1993a, b, 1994a, b, 1995b, 1997b). The increasing algorithmic complexity of an evolving capitalist economy is emphasised.

Chapter 3 formulates *the hypothetical law of motion* of the model economy grasped as the three-dimensional system of nonlinear differential equations. The state variables are capital–output ratio, relative wage and employment ratio. The necessary and sufficient conditions for local stability in the neighbourhood of a non-trivial equilibrium are found. The model is included in the framework of the system dynamics approach outlined by J. Forrester. The interaction of the accelerator and multiplier typically generates cyclical growth in this theoretical framework.

Chapter 4 represents interconnections between the state variables as a competitive–co-operative system. The reference to a richer empirical base and application of more advanced scientific instruments than available to Marx offer new solutions to the problems with which he wrestled. This book argues that Marx's general law of capital accumulation and law of the tendency of the rate of profit to fall should be reconsidered. The author derives formulae showing the constancy of the relative wage, employment ratio and profit rate over the long term. These magnitudes are all the greater, the higher the rate of technological progress.

The stabilising influence of the special form of technological progress on economic dynamics and the destabilising consequences of excessive delays in the adjustment of wage rates are displayed via computer simulations. These experiments uncover pitfalls of involuntary learning in social bargaining.

It is shown that the model is capable of generating long waves and other economic fluctuations in the vicinity of a dynamic equilibrium (steady-state growth path) via the Hopf bifurcation. The internal structure of capital accumulation drives long-wave rhythms. Thus the key relationships are endogenous. The long-run movements of several economic indicators fit into a uniform framework.

The main model variables (the relative wage, employment and capital–output ratios) have no trend. The determination of a secular trend in economic activity, i.e. a general tendency in a specific direction, is a by-product of obtaining the equations of motion for these variables. This approach to the model economy is free from the perspectivistic distortion resulting from a mechanistic detrending of the statistical data that is a characteristic of many empirical studies of Kondratiev's cycles (see Reijnders 1990).

The upswing and downswing phases of the long cycle are determined relative to the steady state for relative quantities (ratios and rates) and in relation to the net output trend. The upswing consists of recovery and prosperity, the downswing embraces recession and depression. These periods are delineated on the basis of movements of the employment ratio that mirror very closely fluctuations of net output around the trend.

Chapter 5 displays the relationships between the profit rate, employment ratio and wage elasticity of demand for labour. The types of control (proportional and derivative), inherent in the model economy, are revealed.

The technological breakthrough in the model is the reaction of entrepreneurs to the downturn. This property of the outlined theory incorporates the view of Schumpeter and G. Mensch that the clustering of innovations causes the Kondratiev cycles. The difference is that such a clustering becomes endogenous instead of being exogenous. An inclusion of scale effects in the model offers a partial explanation for the well-known productivity slowdown in the industrialised capitalist economies since the end of 1960s.

Chapters 3 and 5 analyse the relations between natural, warranted and actual rates of economic growth. Deviations between these rates are born, amplified to a certain maximal level and then eliminated in a recurrent manner in computer simulation runs. As the Russian poet Marina Tsvetaeva says,

The same water–different wave.
What matters is that is a *wave*.
What matters is that the wave *will return*.
What matters is that it *always* returns *different*.
What matters most of all: however different the returning wave,
It always returns as a wave of *the sea*.
What is a wave? Composition and muscle . . .[3]

Chapter 6 exercises the Valtukh taxonomy of societal types depending on social information relationships with nature. An extended model of *eco-capitalism* reflects the impact of economic activities upon natural environmental conditions. These conditions, in their turn, influence the growth rates of labour productivity and capital intensity. A social policy, based on a perception of resource scarcity and pollution levels, is also included in this model. These additions apply the elements of the satellite system for integrated environmental and economic accounting.

A more general statement of a hypothetical law of motion is provided by the set of differential equations of a higher dimensionality. The laws of social motion evolve steadily and their full-blown definition once and for all is avoided. The growing length of mathematical algorithms and computer programs indicates an increasing amount of information required to specify regular features of the complex societal living system.

The steady states of the initial and extended models are compared. It is shown that an economy that cares more about the environment can grow faster and have a higher average ratio of employment than an economy that cares less. The relative wage is also greater, on average, than that in the initial model if the model parameters satisfy the condition specified in this chapter. It is shown that the coefficient of *eco-efficiency* is a control parameter for the equilibrium values of relative wage, employment ratio, capital coefficient and the share of environmental investments in the net domestic product.

The reader's attention is also directed to real problems of reproduction on a decreasing scale in contemporary Russia that is unprecedented in an industrial economy in peacetime in the twentieth century. The country's territorial integrity has been challenged. Her troublesome development is traced back to an unsustainable pattern, generated by the theoretical model. This pattern is brought about by social myopia and, particularly, by reckless attitudes to natural capital.

Thus, this book offers a definite framework for modelling cyclical growth, sustainable development and social policy. It may be useful for training the reader's logic, intuition and creativity necessary for control of nonlinear systems.

The original models have been tested against stylised facts and undergone numerous laboratory experiments. A detailed statistical verification and calibration of these models still remain to be done. Combining algorithmic and probabilistic information is also the subject for future research into control. Unlike the present writing, research into these subject matters will never be finished.

NOTES

1. The reader may compare the diets of a cosmonaut and of an "average" consumer to illuminate this idea.
2. This picture of the American artist E. Vedder (1836–1923) is on show in the Museum of Fine Arts (Boston, Massachusetts).
3. From the essay "Poets with history and poets without history" (Hirsch 1999: 23).

The laws of quantum physics are of a statistical character.
This means: they concern not one single system
but an aggregation of identical systems ...
Quantum physics abandons individual laws
of elementary particles and states *directly*
the ... laws governing aggregations ...

Einstein and Infeld (1938: 300–302)

CHAPTER 1

THE MACROECONOMIC OPERATION OF THE LAW OF VALUE

1.1   VALUE AND PRICE

According to Marx, the magnitude of value of any reproducible commodity is the amount of labour socially necessary for its reproduction.[1] Without going into detail, we will follow Valtukh (1987) to demonstrate a connection between value and its money form — price — in a simplified case. The most important assumptions are the following.

Let private commodity production be such that every branch specialises in manufacturing only one kind of commodity and that all firms are strictly monoproduct ones. The economy is a closed one. It is characterised by a state of market equilibrium. We abstract here from peculiarities of renewable and non-renewable natural resources. Resource rent and natural capital are outside the model boundaries (a relaxation of this assumption is made in Chapter 6).

Differences between price and value are inherent in the price form as such. They allow the law of value to impose itself only as the mean of apparently lawless irregularities that compensate one another. The operation of the law of value includes movements of supply, demand, prices, as well as intra- and inter-industry competition. This mechanism will not be described in this section. It requires special models (see Chapter 2).

The total sum of labour directly and indirectly expended on the production of any product (per year) can be calculated approximately using the following equation:

$$w = l(I_1 - A)^{-1}, \tag{1.1}$$

where $w = (w_1, \ldots, w_n)$ is the row vector of the total labour input coefficients; n is the number of products in the economy, $n \geq 2$; $A = \{a_{ij}\}$ is a quadratic matrix of coefficients of expenditure of the means of production of kind i on producing one unit of commodity of kind j (in other words, a_{ij} is the amount of the ith product required per unit of the jth product); $l = (l_1, \ldots, l_n)$ is a row vector of direct labour input coefficients, $l_j(j = 1, \ldots, n)$ is the direct labour input of the jth product; I_1 is a unit matrix.[2]

Denote the firm's index by k, $k \in E$ — a set of private capitalist firms that actually operate during the given year; $E = \cup E_j$, $j = 1, \ldots, n$, E_j is a set of firms in branch j. Let q_j^k denote the output of commodity j by firm k. Then the output of each branch is

$$q_j = \sum q_j^k > 0, \quad j = 1, \ldots, n.$$

Individual input coefficients by firms are designated by a_{ij}^k, l_j^k, i, $j = 1, \ldots, n$; $k \in E_j$. Then coefficients a_{ij} and l_j are average weighted input quantities; the weights are output volumes q_j^k. For convenience both terms "value" and "magnitude of value" are used as synonyms.

The sum of labour spent to produce a commodity in the kth private firm is called individual value. It is approximated as

$$w_j^k = \sum w_i a_{ij}^k + l_j^k, \quad k \in E_j, j = 1, \ldots, n, \tag{1.2}$$

where a_{ij}^k, l_j^k are direct input coefficients for this firm.

The capitalist mode of production involves a tendency towards fast development of the productive forces and generates strong stimuli to risk taking and innovation. Its aim is to promote self-expansion of capital. Technologies providing individual value lower than the social one ($w_j^k < w_j$) are, as a rule, receiving wide diffusion, while extra surplus value is vanishing, and the social value (w_j) is decreasing.

The law of value as such presupposes net prices are proportional to corresponding direct labour input coefficients:

$$p_j - \sum p_i a_{ij} = v_j = hl_j, \tag{1.3}$$

where p_j is the price of the jth commodity, v_j is its net price, h is a constant for all j, $h > 0$.

The following formula is an expression of the law of value with reference to the dynamics of prices:

$$I v_j = I h I l_j \quad \text{for all } j = 1, \ldots, n, \tag{1.4}$$

where $I v_j$, $I l_j$ are indices of net price and direct labour intensity of commodity j (without regard for the reduction of qualified labour to a simple one), and $I h$ is assumed to be a reflection of inflation. Thus direct proportionality must exist between net prices and labour input coefficients. Hence it is likely that relative net prices drop for commodities of branches with relatively high growth of labour productivity. Fabricant's empirical law reflects this regularity.

The formula (1.4) may be tested statistically. Each branch is treated as one observation, and the movements of the variables are correlated with each other in the form of an inter-industry cross-section analysis.[3] If formula (1.4) is valid, there must be a negative linear correlation between indices of prices and those of labour productivity. Therefore, a linear regression model is appropriate. Its standard form is as follows:

$$y_i = \beta_0 + \beta_1 x_i + u_i \quad (i = 1, \ldots, m), \tag{1.5}$$

where y_i is the ith observation of the dependent variable, x_i is the ith observation of the independent (explanatory) variable, u_i is the ith unobserved disturbance term; β_0 and β_1 denote the constant term and the regression coefficient to be estimated, m is the number of observations (branches).

In what follows we use the same statistical procedure not only for testing the correlation between relative net prices and the relative dynamics of labour productivity but also for a study of inter-industry pattern of growth. All regressions are of the type (1.5).[4]

The link between wage rates and labour productivity is not similar to that between productivity and relative prices. Wage rates in the various sectors of the economy grow at roughly the same rate. This provisional assessment is supported by the relatively small variation in the movement of earnings (see below).

Deviations of prices from value are partly due to market disequilibrium: prices deviate upward or downward from the centre of gravity depending on the extent of excess demand or excess supply. These deviations provide for a redistribution of surplus value produced in slowly growing or even declining industries in favour of fast-growing ones (differences in output growth rates can be expected to reflect the differences in the rates of increase in demand for the output of various industries). In this way relatively fast-growing industries and firms obtain additional resources for their development.

Endogenous technological progress brings about structural changes in the economy which in turn serve as its indicator. The fast-growing industries are usually characterised by rapid technological progress and by above-average increases in labour productivity which in turn cause both relative values and relative prices to fall. This process stimulates demand for the products of these industries; therefore their relative net prices decrease, but at a slower pace than the corresponding values.

The effect of investment in one sector on the profitability of investment in another, via increased demand or reduced costs, has been called by Scitovsky a "dynamic external economy". The imputation of these economies to the originating sectors may seriously affect the estimate of competitive advantage (see Chenery 1961: 21).

Branches facing structural and (or) industrial crises are often not able to stimulate demand even by a sharp absolute or relative reduction in prices of their output. In these cases output growth does not respond directly to price adjustments. "It is in relation to these [declining] industries, where the possibility of expanding demand is limited, that rapid technological progress will lead most directly to technological unemployment" (Freeman, Clark and Soete 1982: 133).

The composition of productive capital is understood in economic science in a twofold sense. In the sense of value, it is determined by the proportion in which it is divided into value of the means of production and value of labour power. It is called value composition of capital. In the sense of material, productive capital is divided into means of production and living labour power. It is the technical composition of capital. Value composition of capital, in so far as it is determined by its technical composition and mirrors the changes in the latter, is called the organic composition of capital (see Marx 1978a: 574).

Marx elaborated the classical theory of price of production for the conditions of free competition. According to this theory, a general rate of profit (average rate of profit) emerges and values of commodities transform into prices of production. The uneven composition of capital in the various branches results, *ceteris paribus*, in a redistribution of surplus value in favour of those branches which have higher than average organic composition of capital. I will return to this issue below.

1.2 CALCULATIONS BASED ON MANUFACTURING DATA

We turn our attention to a statistical analysis of the operation of the law of value under modern capitalism with an application to Austria (see Ryzhenkov 1989). This section deals with the inner relationship between technological advance and the inter-industry pattern of net price dynamics.

The information used in this section is based on the Austrian Annual Census of Manufacturing Establishments, which takes the establishment as its base unit. The data were supplied by the Austrian Institute of Economic Research. They were compiled from industrial statistical surveys which cover all establishments affiliated to the Industry Section of the Chamber of Commerce, but not establishments belonging to the "Small Industry Section". The results do not include any estimates for units not covered by the surveys. The manufacturing branches do not comprise a randomly selected sample from the general population of branches of the economy.

We used two consolidated classifications of industry branches. The first covers 19 branches, the second 10 branches aggregated on the basis of the initial subdivision. The second classification allows us to calculate net prices, whereas the first one does not.

The second classification was built upon the first one in the following way:

1.	Mining	Mining
2.	Petroleum and petroleum products	Petroleum and petroleum products
3.	Basic metal industries	Iron and steel, non-ferrous metals, foundries
4.	Pottery, china, glassware	Stone and clay products, glass and glass products
5.	Chemicals	Chemicals
6.	Paper, paper products	Pulp and paper, paper products
7.	Wood, wood products, furniture	Wood, wood products, furniture
8.	Food, beverages, tobacco	Food, beverages, tobacco
9.	Textiles, apparel, leather	Leather, textiles, apparel
10.	Metal products, machinery, equipment	Machinery, transport equipment, metal products, electrical industry

Calculations were carried out on the basis of production data at 1976 "constant" prices. This means that a fixed weight volume index of output was used with all its well-known shortcomings (it does not take into account the appearance of new products and the disappearance of old ones, etc.). The Austrian statisticians noted that a base for such indices must be changed every five years in order to avoid great statistical distortions (for details see Österreichisches Statistisches Zentralamt 1981).

Labour productivity is defined here as the ratio of output of an industry to its labour input. Output is measured by value added at 1976 constant prices. Labour input is measured by the number of employees.

Data on compensation of employees were taken without any corrections. Data on the number of employees by branches were also accepted without any adjustments. Net price indices were obtained by dividing value added for every branch at current prices by value added at constant prices. Here, a net price presents not only new value created in production by labourers but also depreciation of fixed capital. It thus differs from v_j by depreciation, whose share in total value added is small, as a rule.

In the following we shall approximate $I\,v_j$ by the price index for value added. Estimates of fixed capital used in this study are based on the perpetual-inventory method according to Almon's model (for details see Hahn and Schmoranz 1983 and Hahn 1983).

The year 1975 was the first year of the crisis in the economic cycle, whose upward phase came to an end in 1980. The year 1984 corresponds to the upward phase of the next industrial cycle. This year was the latest one for which data were available at the time of my study at the Austrian Institute for Economic Research. From a long-term point

Table 1.1 Changes over the period 1975–84 for aggregated branches of Austrian industry
$(1975 = 100)^a$

Branch	Labour productivity		Net price		Gross wages and salaries per employee		Unit labour costs	
	1980	1984	1980	1984	1980	1984	1980	1984
1	127.1	146.3	116.0	133.1	144.0	174.5	113.3	119.3
2	93.2	74.0	146.3	205.3	159.9	191.2	171.6	258.4
3	131.2	150.0	118.5	130.2	138.1	171.7	105.3	114.5
4	138.8	158.9	118.8	144.0	148.7	185.5	107.1	116.7
5	130.2	166.5	111.5	108.5	143.9	182.7	110.5	109.7
6	143.0	187.2	121.4	130.4	147.4	191.6	103.1	102.4
7	132.8	139.3	110.6	131.7	145.4	180.3	109.5	129.4
8	121.1	139.7	121.7	135.0	144.0	183.0	118.9	131.0
9	125.9	134.2	122.0	142.2	140.7	179.2	111.8	133.5
10	129.7	156.9	121.6	130.9	143.8	185.0	110.9	117.9
X_j	127.3	145.3	120.8	139.1	145.6	182.5	116.2	133.3
S_{X_j}	13.5	29.5	9.9	25.1	5.9	6.4	20.6	45.0
Var_j	10.6	20.3	8.2	18.1	4.0	3.5	17.2	33.8
$X_j^{\max} - X_j^{\min}$	49.8	113.2	35.7	96.7	21.9	20.0	68.5	156

^{a}The following designations are used in this table and the other similar tables: X_j is an unweighted average, S_{X_j} is a root-mean-square deviation, Var_j is a coefficient of variation (%), $X_j^{\max} - X_j^{\min}$ is a range. *Source*: WIFO data bank.

of view, the whole period 1975–84 belongs to the downswing in the fourth Kondratiev cycle (for details see section 3.5 and Chapter 5).

Before looking at statistical tables, it is necessary to notice that we start with units of measurement used in ordinary language for labour input, productivity and other variables. A. Einstein and L. Infeld (1938: 14) write: "Scientific concepts often begin with those used in ordinary language for the affairs of everyday life, but they develop quite differently. They are transformed and lose the ambiguity associated with them in ordinary language, gaining in rigorousness so that they may be applied to scientific thought." Less ambiguous units of measurement are introduced in section 3.3.

Table 1.1 sets out the dynamics of labour productivity, net prices, gross wages and salaries per person employed, and a number of statistics relating to these variables. Even the first simple comparisons show that the expected statistical relationship between net prices and labour productivity is apt to hold.

Both in the period 1975–80 and in 1975–84 labour productivity rose in all branches except "Petroleum and petroleum products". The highest growth was recorded for "Paper and paper products" (+43 and 87.2%, respectively). For net prices, the branch "Petroleum and petroleum products" posted the highest rate of increase, while commodity prices of the branches "Wood, wood products, furniture" (1975–80) and "Chemicals" (1975–84) showed the lowest increase. In these two branches the rate of labour productivity growth has been higher than the arithmetic mean. In 1984 the price index for "Paper, paper products" was lower than the arithmetic mean but was approximately equal to the mean in 1980.

Coefficients of variation of labour productivity indices exceed those of price indices which in their turn are higher than coefficients of variation of gross wages and salaries per

Table 1.2   OLS regression of net price indices on indices of labour
productivity. Ten branches of Austrian industry[a]

	1975–80	1975–84
Constant term b_0	196.6	246.4
Estimated standard deviation of $b_0(\%)$	10	9
Regression coefficient b_1	−0.595	−0.738
Estimated standard deviation of $b_1(\%)$	25	20
Coefficient of correlation R_{ij}	−0.816	−0.867
Coefficient of determination (R_{ij}^2)	0.666	0.751
Corrected coefficient of determination	0.621	0.714
Standard error of the disturbances	6.04	13.3
t-value of the regression coefficient	−3.99	−4.91
Critical value for the t-distribution under two-sided significance level 0.01	3.169	3.169

[a]Calculated according to Table 1.1.

person employed. A priori one cannot state that the manufacturing branches do represent all branches of the economy. Hence the application of standard statistical procedures for testing the significance of the coefficients is not well grounded. Nevertheless, these procedures have been used (see some results below). The outcome will be compared with other statistical estimations.

Table 1.2 lists the statistical characteristics of the closeness of the relationship between the net price and labour productivity indices. In agreement with the law of value and Fabricant's empirical law, the correlation coefficients are negative; their absolute values are rather high. They seem to be significant at the 1% level of significance.

The null hypothesis $H_0 : R_{ij} = 0$ may be rejected. This conclusion should be considered a provisional one. We applied the ordinary least squares procedure without thoroughly testing for all the necessary conditions for its application, but some additional computations were used in order to verify the OLS estimates. We calculated the values of Spearman's rank correlation coefficients by the formula

$$r_{kj} = 1 - \frac{6S_{kj}(d^2)}{m(m^2 - 1)},$$

where $S_{kj}(d^2)$ is the sum of squared deviations of the ranks of variables. Here m is the number of branches.

The values of r_{kj} for 1975–84 and for 1975–80 are rather high (0.636, 0.6). The a priori probability of obtaining the sum $S \le S_{kj}(d^2)$ is sufficiently small: it equals 0.037 for 1975–80 and 0.030 for 1975–84. So calculations of r_{kj} and Pr $[S \le S_{kj}(d^2)]$ support the rejection of the null hypothesis.

The coefficients of determination (see Table 1.2) equal 0.666 for 1975–80 and 0.751 for 1975–84, while adjusted ones equal 0.621 and 0.714, respectively. In other words, approximately two-thirds of the variations in net prices can be explained (in a purely statistical sense) by movements of labour productivity. In terms of elasticity (evaluated at the mean), an increase in labour productivity of 10% leads to a 6.0 or 7.4% reduction in net prices.

The labour value is, very likely, more real than the smile of the Cheshire Cat, contrary to its (mis)understanding by neo-classical writers! Still Lewis Carroll's *Alice's Adventures*

Table 1.3   OLS regression of indices of gross wages and salaries per employee on indices of labour productivity. Ten branches of Austrian industry[a]

	1975–80	1975–84
Constant term b_0	180.3	185.7
Estimated standard deviation of $b_0(\%)$	8	6
Regression coefficient b_1	−0.273	−0.02
Estimated standard deviation of $b_1(\%)$	44	345
Coefficient of correlation R_{ij}	−0.628	−0.1
Coefficient of determination (R_{ij}^2)	0.394	0.01
Corrected coefficient of determination	0.341	0
Standard error of the disturbances	4.85	6.78
t-value of the regression coefficient	−2.28	−0.29
Critical value for the t-distribution under two-sided significance level 0.01	3.169	3.169

[a]Calculated according to Table 1.1.

in Wonderland is relevant in a general sense as we meet more and more curious enigmas along our rewarding expedition.

Now let us consider indices of wages and salaries per person employed. As was expected, the inter-industry variations in movements of earnings are small. The standard variation (for 1975–80) is 44% of that of labour productivity and 60% of that of prices (for 1975–84 22% and 25%, respectively). There is no indication that an increase in earnings is positively correlated with an increase in labour productivity in the cross-section analysis (see Table 1.3).

The author of this book agrees with W. Salter (1960: 116) that "... in view of the extreme unevenness of productivity movements, any direct link between wages and productivity in individual industries would soon lead to a hopelessly distorted wage structure". Suggestions to link wages and productivity at the industry level therefore appear unrealistic because they contradict this tendency.[5] Wage rates in various sectors of the economy, like labour power values, are mainly determined by general socio-economic factors. A certain segmentation of the labour market also plays a significant role in determining rates of growth of real wages of different qualification groups. The latter are not treated explicitly in this research.

Spearman's rank correlation coefficients between indices of net prices and indices of average gross earnings (in the cross-section analysis) equal 0.13 for 1975–80 and 0.273 for 1975–84. These values are hardly statistically significant. Spearman's rank correlation coefficients between indices of net prices and indices of unit labour costs (in the cross-section analysis) equal 0.5 for 1975–80 and 0.77 for 1975–84. These values are statistically significant.

This significance is based, in my view, on the small inter-industry variations in movements of earnings and the negative correlation between net prices and labour productivity indices. It appears that this explanation may be considered as the alternative to the concept of a "price–wage" spiral that follows from the well-known concept of mark-up pricing. Marx demonstrated that the latter entails a vicious circle in reasoning (see Marx 1970: 21–23).

In order to estimate variations in the organic composition of capital, ratios of fixed capital to persons employed were calculated. Movements in fixed capital per employee show greater diversity than net output per employee. A comparison of the change in the ratios of fixed capital to wages and salaries, on the one hand, with the change in the ratios of net output to gross wages and salaries, on the other, have yielded similar results. Deviations of prices from value are to some extent related to our approximate measures of the organic composition of capital. For example, surplus value tends to stream into the branches "Petroleum and petroleum products" and "Chemicals", which have, according to our estimates, a relatively high organic composition of capital (see Tables 1.4 and 1.5). Spearman's rank correlation coefficient between fixed capital per employed person and net output per gross wages and salaries for 1976 and 1984 equals 0.52 and 0.53, respectively. These values are apparently statistically significant at the 2.5% level of significance. Some additional calculations were carried out in order to investigate the nature of the relationship between prices and the organic composition of capital.

The branches of manufacturing were classified into two groups: the first comprises branches with an above-average ratio of fixed capital to employees, the second those with a below-average ratio. Observations were treated as positive outcomes of statistical

Table 1.4   A test of the relationship between the price and organic composition of capital for 19 branches of Austrian manufacturing. Original aggregation, 1976[a]

		Ratios and their ranks (in parentheses)	
		of fixed capital (at current prices) to employees (million AS per capita)	of value added (at current prices) to gross wages and salaries (dimensionless)
1.	Mining	1.091 (17)	1.563 (5)
2.	Petroleum and petroleum products	2.847 (19)	3.518 (19)
3.	Iron and steel	0.875 (14)	1.836 (11)
4.	Non-ferrous metals	0.931 (16)	2.075 (14)
5.	Stone and clay products	0.923 (15)	1.946 (12)
6.	Glass and glass products	0.497 (8)	1.780 (8)
7.	Chemicals	0.664 (12)	2.289 (16)
8.	Pulp and paper	1.115 (18)	2.000 (13)
9.	Paper products	0.514 (9)	1.783 (9)
10.	Wood, wood products, furniture	0.656 (11)	2.527 (17)
11.	Food, beverages, tobacco	0.724 (13)	3.076 (18)
12.	Leather	0.230 (2)	1.788 (10)
13.	Textiles	0.437 (7)	1.720 (7)
14.	Apparel	0.192 (1)	1.455 (4)
15.	Foundries	0.606 (10)	0.726 (1)
16.	Machinery	0.347 (6)	1.610 (6)
17.	Transport equipment	0.309 (3)	1.309 (3)
18.	Metal products	0.341 (5)	1.169 (2)
19.	Electrical equipment	0.309 (4)	2.281 (15)
	Total industry	0.562 (–)	1.951 (–)

[a]Calculations based on WIFO data bank.

Table 1.5   A test of the relationship between the price and organic composition of capital for 19 branches of Austrian manufacturing. Original aggregation, 1984[a]

	Ratios and their ranks (in parentheses)	
	of fixed capital (at current prices) to employees (million AS per capita)	of value added (at current prices) to gross wages and salaries (dimensionless)
1. Mining	2.000 (17)	1.777 (8)
2. Petroleum and petroleum products	5.747 (19)	2.901 (18)
3. Iron and steel	1.815 (15)	1.886 (9)
4. Non-ferrous metals	1.667 (14)	2.175 (12)
5. Stone and clay products	1.836 (16)	2.125 (11)
6. Glass and glass products	1.179 (9)	2.737 (17)
7. Chemicals	1.266 (10)	2.383 (13)
8. Pulp and paper	3.191 (18)	2.581 (15)
9. Paper products	0.930 (8)	2.073 (10)
10. Wood, wood products, furniture	1.439 (13)	2.673 (16)
11. Food, beverages, tobacco	1.418 (12)	3.047 (19)
12. Leather	0.390 (2)	1.693 (6)
13. Textiles	0.862 (7)	1.730 (7)
14. Apparel	0.356 (1)	1.436 (3)
15. Foundries	1.336 (11)	0.690 (1)
16. Machinery	0.770 (5)	1.368 (2)
17. Transport equipment	0.682 (3)	1.527 (5)
18. Metal products	0.800 (6)	1.437 (4)
19. Electrical equipment	0.713 (4)	2.454 (14)
Total industry	1.156 (−)	2.034 (−)

[a]Calculations based on WIFO data bank.

experiments if a branch from the first group had a ratio of net output to gross wages and salaries that was higher than average or if a branch from the second group had a below-average ratio. Other observations were considered as negative outcomes (see Tables 1.6 and 1.7).

In 1976 and 1984 the expected correspondence held in 14 out of 19 cases (73.7% of all cases). Marx's theory of price of production explains this correspondence in such a way that the price mechanism redistributes surplus value in favour of branches with a higher organic composition of capital.

The outcomes partly reflect the differences in the rates of increase in demand for output of various branches and the degree to which this demand is met (see Tables 1.6 and 1.7). For 1976 the divergence was registered for four branches from the first group ("Mining", "Iron and steel", "Foundries", "Stone and clay products") and for one branch from the second group ("Electrical equipment"). For 1984 the divergence was registered for three branches from the first group ("Iron and steel", "Mining", "Foundries") and two branches from the second ("Paper products", "Electrical equipment").

Thus, surplus value is likely to be redistributed in favour of rapidly expanding branches where supply does not satisfy effective demand, although branches facing a crisis and (or) a depression frequently claimed a bigger share of the sum total of surplus value because of a higher organic composition of capital.

There is a close positive correlation between ratios of net output to gross wages and salaries and the ratios of the value of capital equipment to the number of employees:

Table 1.6   A test of the relationship between the organic composition of capital and price value differences for 19 branches of Austrian manufacturing, 1976[a]

	Branches with a ratio of fixed capital to employees higher than average	Branches with a ratio of fixed capital to employees lower than average
Branches with a ratio of value added to gross wages and salaries higher than average	Petroleum and petroleum products Chemicals Pulp and paper Wood and wood products Food, beverages, tobacco Non-ferrous metals	Electrical equipment
Branches with a ratio of value added to gross wages and salaries lower than average	Mining Foundries Iron and steel Stone and clay products	Leather Textiles Apparel Metal products Machinery Transport equipment Paper products Glass and glass products

[a]Based on Table 1.4.

Table 1.7   A test of the relationship between the price and organic composition of capital for 19 branches of Austrian manufacturing, 1984[a]

	Branches with a ratio of fixed capital to employees higher than average	Branches with a ratio of fixed capital to employees lower than average
Branches with a ratio of value added to gross wages and salaries higher than average	Petroleum and petroleum products Chemicals Pulp and paper Wood and wood products Food, beverages, tobacco Non-ferrous metals Stone and clay products Glass and glass products	Electrical equipment Paper products
Branches with a ratio of value added to gross wages and salaries lower than average	Mining Foundries Iron and steel	Leather Textiles Apparel Metal products Machinery Transport equipment

[a]Based on Table 1.5.

Spearman's rank correlation coefficients for 1974 and 1984 are equal to 0.74 and 0.45. They are significant at the 1% level of significance. These outcomes might be considered a corroboration of the thesis of redistribution of surplus value (and profit) in favour of industries with a relatively high organic composition of capital. Effects of monopolisation on net prices were not uncovered by the author. They need to be investigated further.

Another possible explanation for the higher rate of surplus value in branches with a higher organic composition of capital may be derived from Valtukh's information value hypothesis (for details see section 3.3). According to this hypothesis, the rate of surplus value, other things being equal, grows along with qualification. The higher the qualification, the higher the capital intensity. There is, *ceteris paribus*, a higher labour qualification in branches with a higher organic composition of capital. Value directly taken from nature may also play a role, especially in branches using non-renewable resources (see Chapter 6).

Valtukh's hypothesis questions the necessity of the Marxian notion of price of production in order to explain the price dynamics. It has been applied in the research of price formation for more detailed classification of branches than used in the present book (see Valtukh 1996b).

1.3   HANDLING OF NATIONAL ACCOUNTS STATISTICS

This section uses data on net and gross output at 1976 prices; 1976 was taken as the starting year because in this year there was a change in the statistical method of gross output measurement. The basic data disaggregate the economy into 19 sectors. The sectors "Financing, insurance, real estate and business services", "Social and personal services", "Public administration and defence" do not produce exchangeable goods, they have therefore been excluded from the analysis.[6] Thus our statistical analysis here deals with 16 sectors.

The "Trade" sector was not excluded. It partly performs the function of continuing the process of production and partly the pure function of changing the forms of labour value. The author was not able to separate one from the other.

For each sector estimates of the development of the following indicators were prepared for the years 1976, 1980, 1984:

- economically active population
- fixed capital
- net output
- labour productivity
- unit materials costs
- capital–output ratio
- net price

An explanation of the meanings of these measures may be useful. Volume of net output refers to net output valued at 1976 prices (a fixed weight volume index). Labour productivity is measured as net output divided by the total number of economically active persons (a sum total of employees and self-employed agents).[7] Net price refers to value added per unit of output or, precisely, the value of net output at current prices per unit of output.

Fixed capital was estimated by the method mentioned above. The ratio of capital to net output is called the capital–output ratio and the ratio of fixed capital to economically active persons, capital intensity.

Unit materials costs have been roughly estimated as a ratio of intermediate product (gross output less net output) to gross output. This quantity should be viewed with great caution because the measure as such does not take into account the influences of advancing division of labour on the share of the intermediate products in gross output by branch.[8]

Tables 1.8 and 1.9 list these estimates. The figures given are relative, with 1976 = 100. For the period 1976–84 the following rates of change apply on average: employment

Table 1.8 Growth indicators for 16 sectors of the Austrian economy for 1980 (1976 = 100)[a]

	Economically active population	Fixed capital	Capital intensity	Net output	Productivity	Unit materials costs	Capital–output ratio	Net price
1. Agriculture	85.6	102.6	119.9	108.9	127.2	100.9	94.3	111.6
2. Mining	88.0	98.5	111.9	103.3	117.4	100.8	95.3	118.4
3. Food	97.1	113.5	116.9	116.2	119.6	100.0	97.7	107.7
4. Textiles, apparel	93.1	101.2	108.7	102.7	110.3	100.2	98.5	116.2
5. Wood, wood products	107.0	115.5	108.1	112.1	104.7	100.1	103.2	117.4
6. Paper, publishing	96.2	114.6	119.1	112.6	117.0	100.2	101.8	115.7
7. Chemicals	102.1	113.6	111.3	125.4	122.8	100.5	90.6	108.5
8. Petroleum	100.0	129.1	129.1	95.0	95.0	102.8	135.9	130.8
9. Non-metallic minerals	96.8	110.0	113.7	115.9	119.7	97.3	95.0	110.4
10. Basic metals	103.2	113.5	110.0	116.0	112.5	98.1	97.8	116.5
11. Metal products	104.0	119.2	114.6	125.7	120.9	100.5	94.8	112.5
12. Electricity, gas, water	98.4	112.4	114.2	119.6	121.5	99.7	94.0	116.1
13. Construction	99.8	105.7	105.9	103.3	103.5	106.9	102.3	132.8
14. Trade	105.5	119.9	113.7	110.0	104.3	100.4	109.0	121.6
15. Restaurants and hotels	109.0	130.2	119.4	107.7	98.8	100.6	120.9	139.7
16. Transport and communication	102.2	120.2	117.6	123.0	120.3	99.2	97.7	115.6
X_j	99.3	113.8	114.6	112.3	113.5	100.5	101.8	118.2
S_{x_j}	6.4	9.0	5.7	8.8	9.6	2.1	11.6	9.0
Var_j	6.5	7.9	5.0	7.8	8.5	2.1	11.4	7.6
$X_j^{max} - X_j^{min}$	23.4	31.7	23.2	30.7	32.2	9.6	45.3	32.0

[a]Source: WIFO data bank.

Table 1.9 Various indicators for 16 sectors of the Austrian economy for 1984 (1976 = 100)[a]

	Economically active population	Fixed capital	Capital intensity	Net output	Productivity	Unit materials costs	Capital–output ratio	Net price
1. Agriculture	78.7	103.9	131.9	117.8	149.7	92.6	88.1	113.4
2. Mining	80.8	92.6	114.6	107.2	132.6	98.3	86.4	140.1
3. Food	92.9	122.0	131.3	118.4	127.5	100.0	103.0	131.3
4. Textiles, apparel	80.7	101.6	125.9	98.5	122.1	99.8	103.2	138.4
5. Wood, wood products	104.1	125.2	120.4	113.4	109.0	99.2	110.4	128.5
6. Paper, publishing	88.3	132.4	150.0	124.2	140.8	100.4	106.6	135.2
7. Chemicals	94.8	120.2	126.9	148.0	156.2	101.2	81.2	121.4
8. Petroleum	95.9	136.9	142.8	70.4	73.4	105.2	194.6	242.1
9. Non-metallic minerals	87.4	115.3	132.0	126.0	144.2	94.2	91.5	127.9
10. Basic metals	90.5	119.1	131.6	120.4	133.1	99.3	98.9	131.3
11. Metal products	95.7	140.7	147.1	139.5	145.8	100.6	100.9	134.3
12. Electricity, gas, water	106.3	124.3	117.0	122.4	115.2	104.3	101.5	143.7
13. Construction	87.5	102.0	116.6	90.8	103.8	112.2	112.3	163.0
14. Trade	105.9	139.1	131.4	117.5	111.0	103.2	118.4	139.2
15. Restaurants and hotels	115.7	163.9	141.7	111.4	96.3	101.4	147.1	175.8
16. Transport and communication	103.8	137.1	132.0	134.9	130.0	99.1	101.6	136.5
X_j	94.3	123.5	130.8	116.3	124.4	100.6	109.1	143.9
S_{X_j}	10.6	23.3	10.7	18.8	22.0	4.2	27.4	30.1
Var_j	11.2	18.9	8.2	16.2	17.7	4.2	25.1	20.9
$X_j^{max} - X_j^{min}$	37.0	71.3	35.4	77.6	82.8	18.5	113.3	128.7

[a]Source: WIFO data bank.

decreased by 5.7%, fixed capital rose by 23.5%, fixed capital per head by 30.8%, net output by 16.3%, labour productivity by 24.4%, unit materials costs by 0.6%, capital–output ratio by 9.1% and net prices by 43.9%.

A greater increase in capital intensity than in labour productivity is typical for a downswing in a Kondratiev cycle. Section 5.4 explains this regularity with the help of a model of cyclical growth.

Capital–output ratio shows the greatest diversity: the coefficient of variation equals 25.1%, while that of unit materials costs is the lowest with 4.2%. There is also considerable variation in the movements of labour productivity and of net output. We will see that these variations are reflected in relative prices. Notice that the movements of net prices are much more diverse than those of net output.

The largest increment in net prices was recorded in the "Petroleum" sector (+142.1%), the smallest in the "Agriculture" sector (+13.4%). Labour productivity rose in all sectors, except in "Restaurants, hotels", where the pace of technological advance was relatively slow especially among small entrepreneurs, and in "Petroleum", where prevailing natural conditions for mining apparently got worse. This deterioration was not compensated by technological improvements. In these two sectors labour productivity was down by 3.7 and 26.6%, respectively.

At a first glance, the steady growth of the "Restaurants, hotels" sector contradicts the decrease in labour productivity and the fast increase in net price. In this case demand was probably more influenced by income elasticity than by price elasticity. In general, the less saturated a need, the higher the growth rates of consumption of goods that satisfy it. The whole issue of the evolution of demand over time goes beyond the scope of this book.[9]

1.3.1 The Inter-industry Correlation Analysis

Tables 1.10 and 1.11 display the correlation coefficients, Table 1.12 presents Spearman's rank correlation coefficients between the variables listed above. The close correlation between indices of labour productivity and indices of relative net prices is shown by the coefficients $R_{ij} = -0.84$ and $r_{ij} = -0.78$ for 1976–84 ($R_{ij} = -0.85$ for 1976–80). The goodness of fit is as follows: the ratio of the explained variation to total variation is nearly

Table 1.10   Coefficients of correlation between various indices for 16 sectors of the Austrian economy, 1976–84 (in parentheses for 1976–80)[a]

	Net output	Productivity	Unit materials costs	Fixed capital	Capital–output ratio
Net output	–	0.80 (0.67)	–	–	–
Economically active population	0.16 (0.30)	−0.46 (−0.51)	–	0.84 (0.78)	–
Unit materials costs	−0.43 (−0.52)	−0.62 (−0.45)	–	–	–
Capital–output ratio	−0.70 (−0.64)	−0.87 (−0.85)	–	–	–
Net price	−0.76 (−0.63)	−0.84 (−0.85)	0.56 (0.58)	–	0.94 (0.77)

[a]Results are based on Tables 1.8 and 1.9.

Table 1.11   Coefficients of correlation between various indices for 16 sectors of the Austrian economy, 1967–74 (in parentheses for 1967–73)[a]

	Net output	Productivity	Unit materials costs	Fixed capital	Capital–output ratio
Net output	–	0.39 (0.28)	–	–	–
Economically active population	0.74 (0.81)	−0.33 (−0.33)	–	0.61 (0.59)	–
Unit materials costs	−0.18 (−0.18)	−0.48 (−0.46)	–	–	–
Capital–output ratio	−0.42 (−0.41)	−0.63 (−0.54)	–	–	–
Net price	−0.46 (−0.57)	−0.76 (−0.63)	0.34 (0.01)	–	0.53 (0.63)

[a]Results are based on WIFO data bank.

Table 1.12   Spearman's rank correlation coefficients between various indices for 16 sectors of the Austrian economy, 1976–84 (in parentheses for 1967–73)[a]

	Productivity	Net output	Net price
Economically active population	−0.50 (−0.40)	0.12 (0.64)	–
Capital–output ratio	−0.86 (−0.54)	−0.58 (−0.48)	0.63 (0.53)
Net output	0.75 (0.28)	–	−0.60 (−0.45)
Unit materials costs	−0.60 (−0.68)	−0.25 (−0.36)	0.77 (0.41)
Net price	−0.78 (−0.58)	−0.60 (−0.44)	–

[a]Results are based on WIFO data bank (see also Table 1.9).

71%. Standard errors of the linear regression are 5 and 17% for 1976–84 and 1976–80, respectively.

On average, a differential increase in labour productivity by 10 percentage points leads to a reduction in relative net prices by 8–12 percentage points. It appears that unequal movements of labour productivity are closely associated with savings in the use of resources per unit of net output.

The large increases in labour productivity occur in sectors with large decreases in unit materials cost and capital–output ratio (cf. Tables 1.10–1.12). It is likely that relative net prices decline in those sectors which more rapidly reduce materials costs per unit produced.

For the 16 sectors of the Austrian economy, there is a weak positive correlation between labour productivity and capital intensity: r_{kj} equals 0.19 for 1976–84 and 0.135 for 1967–73.

Exclusion of the sectors extensively using non-renewable resources and the service sector ("Petroleum", "Mining", "Restaurants, hotels") shows that these variables are stronger positively correlated: r_{kj} equals 0.657 for 1976–84 and 0.648 for 1976–80. (I will return to this point in section 3.2.)

Sectors with a more vigorous increase of fixed capital per worker (outside the Austrian extractive industry and services) were able to reap more benefits from technological progress than others. I will consider capital intensity as a macroeconomic factor of labour productivity with the help of Kaldor's technical progress function (see section 3.1).

The close associations between the movements of net output, labour productivity, unit materials cost and capital–output ratio seem to support the existence of economies of scale. These economies could partly explain the general reduction of the unit costs which accompanied the increases in labour productivity.

A comparison of the coefficients which are in parentheses with those which are not (cf. Tables 1.10–1.12) shows that both periods (1976–84 and 1967–74) are characterised by a close correlation between relative net prices and movements of labour productivity. The absolute value of the correlation coefficient grew from 0.76 to 0.84, while the regression coefficient and the standard errors of the regression hardly changed.

While the positive correlation between net output and labour productivity growth (Verdoorn's empirical law) was not strong for 1967–74, it strengthened for the more recent period 1976–84 (cf. Tables 1.10–1.12). There remains, however, a considerable amount of unexplained inter-industry variance in labour productivity growth. It might perhaps be explained by a structural reorganisation of the declining industries, where the most inefficient plants or vintages are closed down, which leads directly to an increase in productivity of the remaining firms as measured by aggregate indices.[10]

The negative correlation revealed between movements of unit materials costs and capital–output ratio, on the one hand, and that of labour productivity, on the other, contradicts the orthodox neo-classical value theory. "If the use of more-specialised machinery is economical only with higher levels of output, there is no reason why a rise in labour productivity should be associated with any fall in capital productivity, but with that explanation, the whole neo-classical value theory clearly goes out of the window", Kaldor wrote (1979: 285–286).

The negative correlation, indicating increasing returns, was more strongly pronounced in the second period (1976–84) than in the first (1967–74). This assertion is also true for the positive correlation between relative growth of net prices and movements of unit materials cost and capital–output ratio. These changes might be interpreted as evidence of an intensification of competition in the Austrian economy during the downswing in the fourth Kondratiev cycle.

In the long run, the labour productivity dynamics of Austrian manufacturing sectors kept pace with those in other industrialised countries: when individual sectors were compared internationally, all but chemicals and basic metals exhibited an above-average performance in the relatively open Austrian economy (see Bayer 1983; Schulmeister, Schebeck and Skolka 1986). The revealed close and positive correlation between differential rates of labour productivity growth and inter-industry net price growth rates in this economy corroborates the conclusion that prices tend to be determined by international value. Evidence of severe price competition supports this thesis. There is also good agreement between empirical findings of this research and F. Rahmeyer's conclusions on price dynamics in German manufacturing industry during 1961–85 (see Rahmeyer 1991).

It is well known that the battle of competition is fought by lowering commodity prices and that this fall in prices is brought about by technological progress and economies of scale. Competition and relative price changes are clearly the driving forces of economic growth; these forces, in turn, are inherent in the law of value and other immanent laws of capitalist production. But international application of these principles should become the object of special investigation.

Bruckmann and Fleissner have estimated a Cobb–Douglas production function on an empirical base. Taking GDP and fixed assets at 1976 prices and the number of employees for 1964–80, they estimated the function

$$\ln Y = a \ln K + b \ln L + c$$

by the OLS method (Bruckmann and Fleissner 1989: 28–30).

According to the orthodox neo-classical school coefficients a and b should be less than 1 and greater than 0 to measure the income shares of capital and labour. In fact, the coefficient at $\ln L$ is negative, contrary to neo-classical postulating.

If, instead of using logarithms, one takes growth rates, the result is not better than with the former. This time the coefficient for capital is negative. The analysis of variation shows in addition very low magnitudes of correlation coefficients. These findings support the theoretical approach to economic growth applied in this book.

For a rather consolidated classification of branches, there has been a close agreement between prices and labour values of produced commodities in the USA for the period 1948–81 (see Valtukh 1987). We have seen that this agreement is also very probable for Austria with its relatively open economy. The universal principles of the theory of value will be used as the base for the theory of economic cyclical growth in the following chapters.

NOTES

1. In this book certain terms are used in a sense that differs from that in neo-classical economics. For example, value is used in the sense of labour value or abstract labour embodied in commodities and not in the sense of exchange value, interchangeable with price.
2. The matrix A is considered to be productive. In this case all elements of matrix $(I_1 - A)^{-1}$ are non-negative, $w_j > l_j > 0$ for all j.
3. A similar formal approach was employed by W. Salter and other economists.
4. The following criterion was used for testing a hypothesis of normal distribution of errors: $1.10 > \sigma/(1.253 \cdot \eta) > 0.90$, where σ is a standard deviation and η is an average linear deviation (see Lisichkin 1971: 102–103). This requirement is satisfied in the above linear regression model of net prices and productivity for 10 branches of Austrian industry (see section 1.2). W. Salter discussed four possible kinds of statistical problems: (i) skewed distributions of the observations which could make the results depend unduly upon extreme cases, (ii) deficiencies in the extent to which the sample is representative, (iii) the ratio form of the correlation, and (iv) errors of measurement (see Salter 1960: 109–113). These questions are not considered in detail in this book.
5. See also *Europäische Wirtschaft*, 1986, No. 29, pp. 125–128.
6. Remember that the Marxian law of value is that of prices.
7. This fraction distorts the actual quantity somewhat because the denominator includes persons who do not perform one of the subordinate functions of a collective labourer (i.e. they are not productive labourers). A proper account of these persons would be desirable, but it was not done in this paper. It is appropriate to regard this estimate and similar ones as indications of the order of magnitude rather than of the magnitude itself.

8. This problem is touched upon in Skolka (1984) and Skolka and Mitter (1984).
9. This issue was partly considered in Valtukh and Ryzhenkov (1981).
10. It is the so-called structural reorganisation hypothesis advanced in Wragg and Robertson (1978). There is evidence that the relationship between movements of net output and those of employment weakened (see Tables 1.10–1.12). See a discussion of this relationship in: Skolka (1984), Skolka and Mitter (1984), Freeman, Clark and Soete (1982) and Wragg and Robertson (1978).

The profound affinity between play and order
is perhaps the reason why play ...
Play has a tendency to be beautiful ...
The element of tension in play ... means uncertainty ...

Johan Huizinga (1950: 10)

CHAPTER 2

COMPETITION, CO-OPERATION AND DIFFUSION OF INNOVATIONS

2.1   A BACKGROUND MODEL OF UNIVERSAL COMMODITY PRODUCTION

To provide a more visual exposition of the law of value operation it is necessary to connect macro- and microeconomic levels. Trade secrets complicate investigations of individual values and costs for an outside expert. My experience in a consulting firm has taught me that managers and industrialists consider their investment strategy as an internal matter. It is mandatory for consulting firms to guarantee a client's trade secrets.

Being restricted by written and unwritten rules of the real world, we can, fortunately, create artificial worlds and rules.[1] The case studies in a university classroom reveal the hand of *Homo ludens*: "It seems to me that next to *Homo Faber*, and perhaps on the same level as *Homo sapiens*, Homo ludens, man the player, deserves a place in our nomenclature" (Huizinga 1950: ix). I will report below results of three representative computer-supported gaming experiments conducted at Novosibirsk State University. Via experiments, students uncover unintended social consequences of individual actions and discuss controversial economic problems.

The Valtukh model, applied in this book, has been designed for gaming experiments and to be used in a classroom.[2] It reflects interconnections between the technological and socio-economic sides of the capitalist mode of production. This model describes relationships between desired and "actual" purchases, prices, investments, production capacities, output and inventory levels for three branches of the economy.

The model is built on input–output tables with technological modes (every firm disposes of an elementary technology). A specification of adjustments taking place by means of price changes and by quantitative rationing is also included.

Demand is a relatively autonomous element of capitalist reproduction. Production capacities are not necessarily operated in full. Capitalists and workers are allowed to save. The labour supply is assumed to be constant. Transaction costs are ignored.

We will analyse voluntary learning within the class of capitalists. Our focus will be feedback loops between micro- and macro-levels. The study shows that the applied theoretical framework can lead to propositions deduced or derived empirically in industrial economics.

Note the other most relevant assumptions. Natural resources are not scarce and supply of homogenous labour power is fixed. At the very beginning of the game players having been endowed with money capital await its application. There are three mono-product sectors. Each kind of commodity can be produced by three or fewer technological modes. Every elementary technique can belong to different capitalists, but initially there are nine capitalists possessing nine firms with respective elementary techniques. Technological modes diffuse here endogenously through the expansion of the innovative firms and through imitation by other firms. Diffusion of innovations adopted by private producers takes place under conditions of market disequilibrium. The model does not take into account patenting and product innovations. Inventions and process innovations that occurred in the past are not considered explicitly.

A capitalist is allowed to construct a "new" firm with any given technique. There is no problem if the capitalist has only one "old" firm. However, if the capitalist has two "old" firms, creation of a "new" firm requires giving up at least one "old" firm and losing fixed assets. Stocks of raw materials from closed firms may be productively consumed. Firms cannot change the mix of products made in their existing plants or diversify production.

A capitalist enters a sector only through construction of a new single-plant firm. These conditions imply the administrative market-entry and market-exit restriction. Players (the capitalists) are informed about magnitudes of parameters in the basal (zero) year: prices of commodities, and profitability of technological modes calculated at these prices. Workers' decisions are reduced to determining a demand for consumer goods. This determination is carried out and processed automatically by a computer program.

The structure of output in the basal year was such that commodities were sold at prices of production providing equal (positive) profit rates in all (three) sectors. The reproducible resources were fully utilised. Workers bought necessary consumer goods to satisfy their normal needs.

At the same time in that idealised situation there were also disequilibrium elements. It is, perhaps, sufficient to mention here different magnitudes and composition of individual advanced capital, unequal profitability of firms and of techniques. Due to these (and to some other) elements the economy develops, giving rise to new combinations of opposite tendencies.

The deep source of nonlinearity in the model is technological progress. Although all techniques are characterised by fixed input coefficients and constant returns to scale at optimal combinations of inputs, a production possibility set is not a convex cone since the constraint of labour supply excludes a limitless expansion of existing plants.[3] The division of investment into intensive and extensive, opening and closing of firms, disproportion of reproduction are immediate factors of nonlinearity.

Possible paths of evolution are not absolutely predetermined by the initial conditions and by the rules of the game, in spite of all equations of the model having a purely deterministic form. The point is that personal selective decision-making introduces stochastic elements in reproduction of capital. A bifurcation can occur at each situation, depending on the concrete decisions of economic agents.

Undertaking an investment, a capitalist firm typically chooses that technique which improves profitability, whereas society is interested in that which requires the smaller input of labour. So it is likely that in the model economy social and private benefits (costs) diverge. In actual practice of advanced capitalism, a state technology policy addresses this problem.

The aim of the capitalist mode of production is to promote self-expansion of capital, but methods by which it accomplishes this imply depreciation of existing capital, stoppages and crises in reproduction. This contradictory development was also pronounced in our experiments.

2.2   THE FIRST GAMING EXPERIMENT

Recent developments in Russia were partially foreseen at Novosibirsk State University in 1989–91 in gaming experiments with the model of a capitalist economy. Students starting to learn economic theory took part in the first game. Decision-making was decentralised. Being inexperienced in the functioning of a capitalist economy, they did not accomplish effective economic growth.

Production was disproportional and very prodigal with its human and material resources. Technical and economic efficiency of the economy was extremely low. From the fourth year to the ninth year, the operating rate was not higher than 25% in the first sector and 38% in the second (see Figures 2.1–2.4). The rate of unemployment increased to 70–79% (years 5, 7–9), and more than 68% of employees were inactive (see Figure 2.5).

Over nine years 69 investment projects were carried out, including 42 (61%) aimed at an extension of given production capacities, 10 (14%) connected with opening of new firms by extant capitalists, and 17 (25%) represented new entrants. It is noteworthy that nearly two-thirds of the number of all projects were intended for extended reproduction of existing firms.

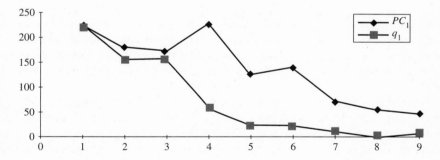

Figure 2.1   Output (q_1) and production capacity (PC_1) in the first sector. The first game

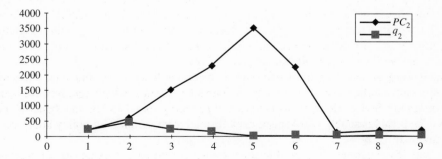

Figure 2.2   Output (q_2) and production capacity (PC_2) in the second sector. The first game

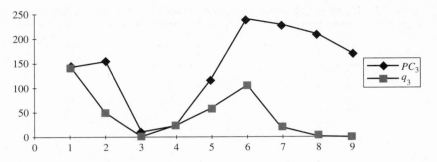

Figure 2.3   Output (q_3) and production capacity (PC_3) in the third sector. The first game

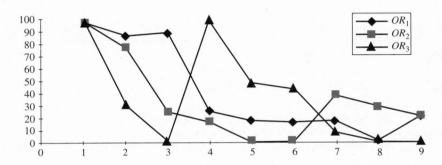

Figure 2.4   The operative rates in the three sectors. The first game

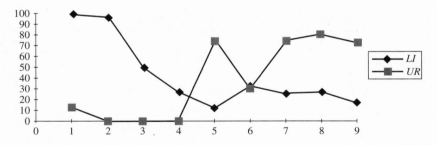

Figure 2.5   The unemployment ratio (UR) and the ratio of the actual labour input to the potential labour input (LI). The first game

We think this behaviour follows from the necessity of compensating for the advanced capital embodied in factory buildings, machinery and equipment. Moral depreciation of fixed capital results from unequal profitability of technological modes in every sector. Fixed assets of less profitable modes should be considered morally obsolete. By closing a firm its owner usually suffers losses if capital cost amortisation is far from being completed. In addition, there is the important restriction in this game: an owner of two firms loses fixed assets of one or two of them at his discretion after investing in new technology.

Table 2.1   Ranks of technologies according to their profitability (the first game)

Technique	Year									Rank	
	0	1	2	3	4	5	6	7	8	Total	Final
1	3	4	4	2	6	5	3	3	3	33	1.5
2	5	5	6	3	5	4	1	2	2	33	1.5
3	8	7	5	4	4	6	2	1	1	38	3
4	9	9	9	5	3	3	9	9	9	65	9
5	6	8	8	1	2	2	7	7	8	49	7.5
6	1	6	7	6	1	1	8	8	7	45	4
7	2	1	1	7	9	9	6	6	6	47	6
8	7	3	3	9	7	7	4	4	5	49	7.5
9	4	2	2	8	8	8	5	5	4	46	5

Still entrepreneurs can try to set off a loss by means of new endeavours. Tables 2.1 and 2.2 list ranks of technologies according to both indicators (a profitability level and number of investment projects engaged). Spearman's rank correlation coefficient between final ranks was equal to 0.55 (connections were disregarded). This magnitude seems to be significant. I would add that new entrants did not choose any technological mode with the lowest profitability inside a sector.

Table 2.3 sets out data on the relative profitability of the sectors. A flow of capital to sectors with higher profitability was illustrated by the fact that final ranks of sectors ordered according to their profitability, on the one hand, coincided with ranks of these sectors ordered according to cumulated net investments, on the other.

Sectoral profitability was also congruent with corresponding firm turnover: the higher the profitability, the higher either opening or closing rates were (see Table 2.4). This

Table 2.2   Distribution of investment projects

Technique	Year									Rank	
	1	2	3	4	5	6	7	8	9	Total	Final
1	1		1	1		1			1	5	3.5
2		1			1		1			3	1
3	2	2	1	1	1					7	6
4	3	2	3	1	1	1	4	1	2	18	9
5			2	2			1	1	2	1	9	7
6		1	1	2	1		3	1	3	12	8
7					2	2				4	2
8	2			3		1				6	5
9	1		1	1	1	1				5	3.5

Table 2.3   Ranks of sectors according to their profitability

	Year									Rank	
	0	1	2	3	4	5	6	7	8	Total	Final
Sector 1	2	2	2	1	2	1	1	1	1	13	1
Sector 2	2	3	3	2	1	2	3	3	3	22	3
Sector 3	2	1	1	3	3	3	2	2	2	19	2

Table 2.4   Firm turnover over nine years (ranks in parentheses)

	Initial number of firms	Number of openings	Number of closings	Number of firms in the ninth year
Sector 1	3	5 (1)	6 (1)	2 (1)
Sector 2	3	14 (3)	9 (3)	8 (3)
Sector 3	3	8 (2)	7 (2)	4 (2)
Total	9	27	22	14

finding tentatively suggests profitability as the characteristic of industry that gives rise to across industry differences in turnover (cf. Dunne, Roberts and Samuelson 1988).

A deficiency of resources and/or a low profitability was declared to be the immediate reason behind firms closing. Players preferred a partial closing of business with redistribution of resources in favour of more profitable sectors to a complete closing of their firms.

Despite these signs of individual rationality, the economy experienced severe crises and decline. The viable technical change was mostly retrogressive, as direct and total inputs of labour per unit of output were increasing (see Figure 2.6).

Technologies 3, 5 and 9 posted the lowest individual labour values for the respective sectors. These technologies still attracted only 21 investment projects (30%) out of 69. On the other hand, the sixth technology, which was socially most ineffective (the value of its output hardly covered the relating production costs in labour value terms), attracted 12 investment projects. These facts illustrate collective irrationality again.

The behaviour of the sixth capitalist deserves mention. He forestalled his competitors investing in the third sector in the third year and got an extra profit two years later. The reduced supply of products from the third sector brought about very low capacity utilisation in the other sectors. Transferring capital to this sector other players miscalculated. More than 50% of its production capacity was not used from the fifth year until the end of the game.

The experiments illustrated the positive dependence of real wages on accumulation of capital (disinvesting resulted in a dramatic decline of employees' living standards). This outcome reminds us of Marx's conclusion that wage is a function of capital accumulation. By buying cheap labour power capitalists were not interested in labour-saving technical progress.

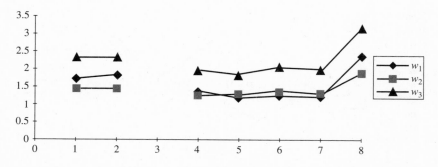

Figure 2.6   The total labour intensities in the three sectors. The first game

2.3   THE SECOND GAMING EXPERIMENT

This case study displays the improved outcome. Participants in the second game were students learning economic theory at a more advanced level. The most active of them have also taken part in the third experiment (see the next section). The second gaming experiment encompasses nine years.

Disequilibrium *lato sensu*, already present in the initial situation, reproduced itself. Demand for elements of fixed assets for investing in existing and in new firms rocketed. However, the productive capacities of the second sector producing elements of fixed assets and stocks of the respective goods were too limited to match the increased demand. This disparity motivated the expansion of this sector amplified by self-ordering (see Figure 2.8). The production capacities tended to expand until output caught up with demand (see Figures 2.7–2.9; cf Sterman 1985: 18–21). The operative rates were higher than in the first game (cf. Figures 2.10 and 2.4).

In each succeeding time interval the capacity (the "hunter") overshoots the previous demand (the "running wild boar") then falls below in the next year in trying to correct the earlier overshoot. The demand, in its turn, is affected by these changes in capacities (our "wild boar" reacts against the "dangerous hunter"). The amplitude of recurrent fluctuations of capacity is greater than that of demand. Excessive time delays in the feedback loops as well as abrupt attempts to correct the discrepancies shape such behaviour (cf. Forrester 1976: 2-2). The observed surplus capacities would probably be even greater if the lifetime of the productive assets was longer than the one year fixed in this sector.

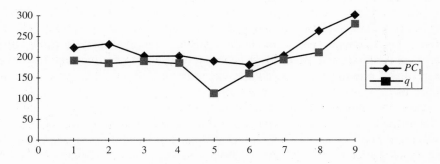

Figure 2.7   Output (q_1) and production capacity (PC_1) in the first sector. The second game

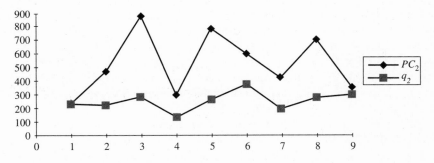

Figure 2.8   Output (q_2) and production capacity (PC_2) in the second sector. The second game

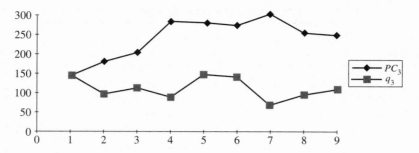

Figure 2.9   Output (q_3) and production capacity (PC_3) in the third sector. The second game

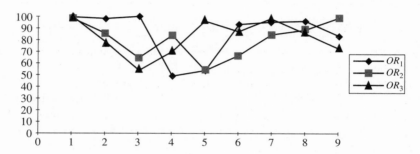

Figure 2.10   The operative rates in the three sectors. The second game

The general economic decline in the middle of the game forced players to develop centralised crisis management (co-ordination costs have been disregarded). In particular, they agreed to stimulate final demand by hiring excessive labour power. This strategy of "benevolent" commodity producers proved to be successful, although it went beyond capitalist social relations in their pure form. (Returning to the risky metaphor, I could imagine that the "hunter" almost tamed the "wild boar".)

In each sector there is a dominant technology which has the greatest rate of profit. Dominated methods have either been eliminated or suppressed while dominant techniques have diffused within established sectors through new capital investment. The ranking of technological modes depending on their profitability is characterised by stability for each sector but not for the economy as a whole (see Table 2.5). Technique 3 is the most profitable in the first sector, technique 4 in the second and technique 8 in the third.

A blank in Table 2.6 means that the respective technique is not used in the year of account. Table 2.5 contains magnitudes for both kinds of technologies (applied and with-drawn) since all these data are relevant for decision-making.

These choices of techniques bring about some inefficiency from the social point of view since the most profitable methods are not necessarily the most labour-saving. A ranking of techniques according to profitability diverges from their inverse ranking according to individual labour values (cf. Tables 2.5 and 2.6).

The dominant (third) technology is the most labour-saving only in the first sector. Technologies 8 and 9 also had close levels of profitability and total labour intensity. Their shares in gross output of the third sector oscillated for the whole period of the game; the most socially effective (ninth) technology did not win the contest.

Table 2.5   Ranks of technologies according to their profitability (the second game)

| Technique | Year | | | | | | | | | Rank | |
	0	1	2	3	4	5	6	7	8	Total	Final
1	3	4.5	4	4	4	4	4	4	2	33.5	3
2	5	6	5	5	5	5	5	5	4	45	5
3	8	7	6	6	6	6	6	6	6	57	7
4	9	9	9	9	9	9	9	9	9	81	9
5	6	8	8	8	8	8	8	8	8	70	8
6	1	2	7	7	7	7	7	7	7	52	6
7	2	1	1	1	1	1	1	1	1	10	1
8	7	4.5	3	3	3	3	3	3	5	34.5	4
9	4	3	2	2	2	2	2	2	3	22	2

Table 2.6   Ranks of technologies according to the total labour intensity (the second game)

| Technique | Year | | | | | | | | | |
	0	1	2	3	4	5	6	7	8	9
1	3	3	3							
2	2	2	2	2	2	2	2	2	2	2
3	1	1	1	1	1	1	1	1	1	1
4	2	2	2	2	1	1	1	1	1	1
5	1	1	1	1						
6	3	3	3	3						
7	3	3	3	3	3	3	3	3	3	3
8	1	1	1.5	2	2	2	2	2	2	2
9	2	2	1.5	1	1	1	1	1	1	1

Capitalists of the second sector preferred the most profitable (fourth) technology to the most progressive (fifth) one. Figure 2.11 graphs diffusion of the fourth technique inside the second sector, producing elements of fixed assets and consumer goods. The picture reminds us of the well-known S-shaped form familiar to researchers of diffusion (cf. Mansfield 1961; Silverberg, Dosi and Orsenigo 1988). The similar S-shaped trajectories characterise the diffusion of the third technology in the first sector.

The players' investment projects are subject to trial and error. The bounded rationality of players is reflected in Figure 2.11 where the output share of the fourth technology declines in the second year.

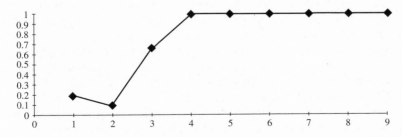

Figure 2.11   The diffusion of the fourth technology measured as its share in the second sector output (q_2^4/q_2). The second game

Over nine years 45 investment projects were carried out. A quantity of engaged investment projects appears to be correlated with technology profitability: Spearman's correlation coefficient (between final ranks) is equal to 0.59 (connections are disregarded). Note that investors (including new entrants) did not choose any technological mode with the lowest profitability inside a sector (modes 1, 6, 7). The relative efficiency of a technological mode is to a great extent invariant to changes in prices and values of commodities.

For the period of the game, the total value of advanced capital increased by 18%, having been reduced in years 2, 4 and 5. Only four capitalists became richer, the other five agents were not so lucky and their advanced capital decreased in value terms. The process of concentration of capital has been rather monotonous judging by its total labour value and by the Herfindahl–Hirschman index, the sum of all the capitalists' squared capital shares, respectively (see Figures 2.12 and 2.13).

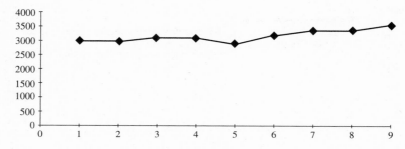

Figure 2.12   The sum total of advanced capital (K_t). The second game

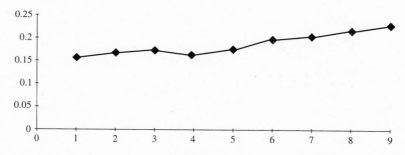

Figure 2.13   Concentration of advanced capital (H_t). The second game

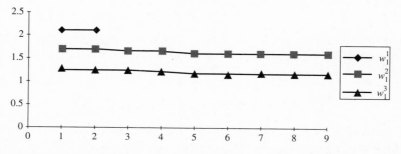

Figure 2.14   The individual total labour intensities in the first sector. The second game

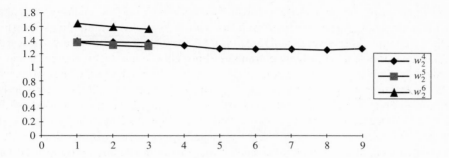

Figure 2.15   The individual total labour intensities in the second sector. The second game

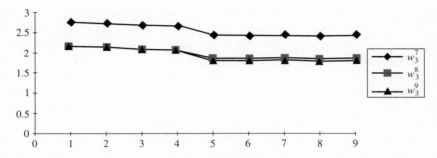

Figure 2.16   The individual total labour intensities in the third sector. The second game

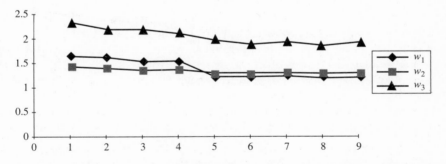

Figure 2.17   The social total labour intensities in the three sectors. The second game

In contrast to the first game, there was a visible technical progress. The latter has manifested itself in the dynamics of individual and social values (see Figures 2.14–2.17).

2.4   THE THIRD GAMING EXPERIMENT

More experienced students modified not only strategies but also norms of behaviour by moving from single-loop to double-loop learning (cf. Argyris and Schön 1978: 18–29). Figure 2.18 displays its general structure.

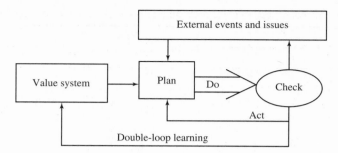

Figure 2.18   A general structure of double-loop learning. Adapted from Argyris and Schön (1978: 18–29)

The third case study illustrates how the players improved their results from the previous ones. The game consists of 11 rounds. Although the initial conditions are the same, technical and economic efficiency is higher than in the previous case (cf. Figures 2.7–2.17 and 2.19–2.28).

The players move into technologies and out of inferior ones faster and more effectively (timing, selection, obsolescence) than in the second game. In particular, they have got rid of technologies 1, 2, 6 and 7 which hinder economic growth (cf. Tables 2.6 and 2.8). The diffusion curves for technologies 3, 4 and 8 are characterised by more rapid and severe increases during the early phases than in the previous experiment (for example, compare Figures 2.23 and 2.11). Capitalists of the second sector this time preferred the most progressive (fifth) technology to the most profitable (fourth) one at the end of the ninth year (see Tables 2.7 and 2.8).

However, the operative rates in the third game do not differ substantially from those of the second (cf. Figures 2.22 and 2.10). The striking improvement occurred in labour force utilisation compared with the first game (cf. Figures 2.24 and 2.5).

In agreement with the classical theory of value, relative prices finally drop for sectors with the higher rates of growth of labour productivity (see Table 2.9). In spite of the continuous modified reproduction of oligopoly structures, prices tend to move in the long run in accordance with labour values.

The game participants recounted that the third game can be divided into two connected stages: the first takes place during years 1–6, the second during years 7–11. An economic

Table 2.7   Ranks of technologies according to their profitability (the third game)

| Technique | Year | | | | | | | | | | | Rank | |
	0	1	2	3	4	5	6	7	8	9	10	Total	Final
1	3	4	3	2.5	5	4	1	2	4	4	2	34.5	3
2	5	6	5.5	6	6	5	2	4	5	5	3	52.5	4
3	8	7	7	7	7	6.5	4	5	6	7	7	63.5	6
4	9	9	9	9	9	9	9	6	3	3	9	84	9
5	6	8	8	8	8	8	8	3	2	2	8	69	8
6	1	1	2	2.5	4	6.5	3	1	1	1	6	29	1
7	2	2	1	1	1	1	5	7	7	6	1	34	2
8	7	5	5.5	5	3	3	7	9	9	9	5	67.5	7
9	4	3	4	4	2	2	6	8	8	8	4	53	5

Table 2.8   Ranks of technologies according to total labour intensity (the third game)

Technique	Year											
	0	1	2	3	4	5	6	7	8	9	10	11
1	3	3	3	3	2	2						
2	2	2	2	2								
3	1	1	1	1	1	1	1	1	1	1	1	1
4	2	2	2	2	2	2	2	2	2	2		
5	1	1	1	1	1	1	1	1	1	1	1	1
6	3	3	3									
7	3	3	3	3	3							
8	1	2	1	2	2	2	2	2	2	2	2	2
9	2	1	2	1	1	1	1	1	1	1	1	1

Table 2.9   The relationship between net price (v_j^t), labour intensity (l_j^t) and gross output (q_j^t) in the second game (over years 1–9) and in the third game (over years 1–11). Ranks in parentheses

	Index for game 2			Index for game 3		
	v_j^9/v_j^1	l_j^9/l_j^1	q_j^9/q_j^1	v_j^{11}/v_j^1	l_j^{11}/l_j^1	q_j^{11}/q_j^1
Sector 1	0.8 (1)	0.6 (1)	1.4 (3)	0.6 (1)	0.5 (1)	1.8 (3)
Sector 2	1.9 (3)	1.6 (3)	1.2 (2)	3.2 (3)	0.9 (3)	1.3 (1)
Sector 3	1.0 (2)	0.9 (2)	0.7 (1)	0.7 (2)	0.89 (2)	1.4 (2)

crisis in the sixth year establishes a border between these stages (see Figures 2.19–2.21). At the end of the sixth round the players decided to co-ordinate their behaviour closely in order to achieve reproduction on an increasing scale.

After some kind of Schumpeterian creative destruction, our players used only the most socially effective technologies (3, 5, 8 and 9) by the end of the game (see Tables 2.7 and 2.8). Figure 2.23 plots the diffusion curve of the fourth technique inside the second sector. This technology was removed in the ninth year, making room for the most socially effective fifth technology. It is noteworthy that the growth over time in the percentage of firms having introduced the fifth technology conforms to the S-shaped growth curve. The slower a sector grows, the slower the rate of imitation (see Table 2.10).

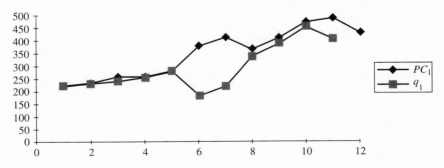

Figure 2.19   The output (q_1) and production capacity (PC_1) in the first sector. The third game

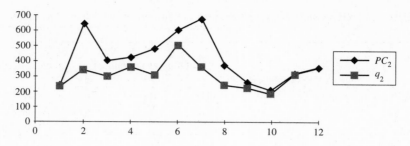

Figure 2.20   The output (q_2) and production capacity (PC_2) in the second sector. The third game

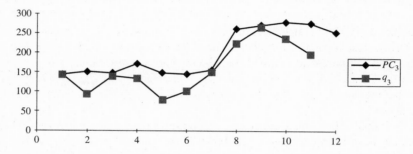

Figure 2.21   The output (q_3) and production capacity (PC_3) in the third sector. The third game

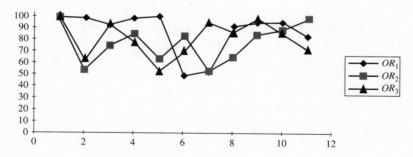

Figure 2.22   The operative rates in the three sectors. The third game

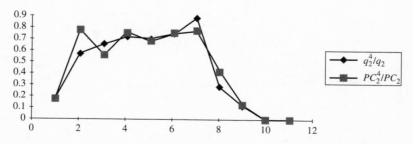

Figure 2.23   The shares of the fourth technology in the output (q_2^4/q_2) and production capacity
(PC_2^4/PC_2) in the second sector. The third game

Table 2.10 The relationships between imitation, concentration and growth for the period 1–11 in the third game

	Gross output (q^t_j)			Imitators at the end of the 11th year		Concentration of production in the 11th year	
	Year 11	Index	Rank	Total	Rank	The Herfindahl–Hirschman index H^t_j	Rank
Sector 1	402.2	1.8	3	7	3	0.23	1
Sector 2	307.3	1.32	1	3	1	0.41	3
Sector 3	195.0	1.36	2	4	2	0.40	2

Horizontal parts of the trajectories displayed on Figures 2.25–2.28 mean that the potential for further diminishing of total labour intensities is almost exhausted. Adoption of the more effective technological system brings the technological frontier nearer. The need for new innovations and for their adoption has been perceived more acutely than ever before. It is notable that Japan, once the main rapid imitator, has become the leader in a variety of innovations.

The Herfindahl–Hirschman indices of concentration of production for three sectors of the economy have been calculated (see Table 2.10). The idea that a closer technical race tends to keep concentration down seems quite plausible as the hypothesis (cf. Nelson and Winter 1982: 232).

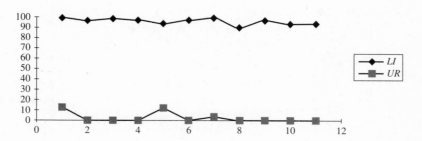

Figure 2.24 The unemployment ratio (UR) and the ratio of the actual labour input to potential labour input (LI). The third game

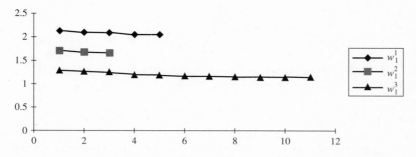

Figure 2.25 The individual total labour intensities in the first sector. The third game

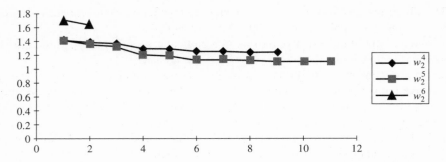

Figure 2.26   The individual total labour intensities in the second sector. The third game

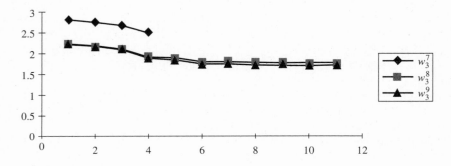

Figure 2.27   The individual total labour intensities in the third sector. The third game

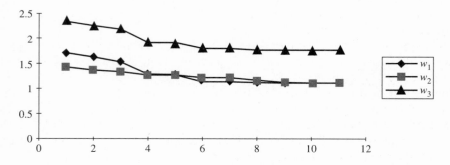

Figure 2.28   The total labour intensities in the three sectors. The third game

Similar indices have also been calculated for estimating concentration of supply and demand. With their help we come to the following very tentative observations in cross-section consistent with the hypotheses often advanced in industrial economics:

- The greater the relative overall rate of growth of output, the greater the number of imitators and the higher the average operating rate in this sector
- The higher the profit rate in a sector, the greater the number of firm openings, on the one hand, and of firm closings, on the other, and the higher the concentration of supply

- The lower the profitability of a sector, the more intensive the propensity to restrict production and supply of commodities among capitalists
- The longer the lifetime of fixed assets in a particular sector, the higher the barriers to exit that sector.

Our data do not warrant the hypothesis that the rate of imitation is higher in more competitive industries (cf. Mansfield 1961: 753). There was some apparent tendency for this rate to be lower in sectors with a longer lifetime of fixed assets, but it was difficult to isolate the influence of this factor from the influence of others.

In the experiment, *ceteris paribus*, the monopolistic tendency was brought about by competitive advantages of firms with the most effective technological modes, which obtained extra profits. The opposite tendency had at least two origins: the ease of imitation (extra profits are eroded by imitators) and the recognition of the fact by extant firms with large market shares that further expansion could spoil their own markets (cf. Nelson and Winter 1982: 280–295).

It was pointed out in the literature that while technological diffusion tends to wither away inter-firm asymmetries, the process of innovation keeps creating new ones (see Dosi 1986: 295; cf. Iwai 1984). Differences between firms' productivity levels have had a tendency to disappear over time in our second and third experiments. The abstraction from innovations during the model period has influenced the outcomes of the experiments. Although our experiments exaggerate the "entropic tendency" towards technological uniformity, they also contain a "negentropic tendency".

The players not only reveal the information embodied in the initial conditions and rules (as participants of J. H. Conway's game "Life" do), but create new information. Their decision-making provides the higher economic order. They keep in mind the choices of techniques by giving preference to the definite connections between different technologies among the broader set of possibilities and generate new behavioural algorithms, thus raising the functional efficiency. Additional information from outside (for example, teaching) accelerates the progressive evolution.

The players have understood the necessity for more co-operative behaviour in order to overcome the crisis and seen the benefits of incurring short-term losses in profitability in order to accrue long-term gains.

From my point of view, deviation from the spontaneous market economy may be considered as a particular manifestation of the tendency towards a higher level of self-organisation. In reality, the transformation of behavioural norms usually implies power shifts and requires a new institutional structure. Strong resistance from powerful groups can delay the necessary reforms for a long time.

In the current global environment, effective technology management is often called the hidden competitive advantage. Our gaming experiments are intended to assist students in making the management of technology clearer and more transparent.

2.5 PRACTICAL IMPLICATIONS

Market relations did not provide a stimulus to technological progress under deep imbalances of reproduction in the first case study. Neither the "invisible hand" nor the "visible foot" helped our aggressive and short-sighted players to utilise fully the potential of this economy. National income narrowed down as compared with the initial one. Small profits, perhaps, also contributed to non-co-operative behaviour of players. Viable technical change was not socially progressive. However, practice is the best teacher.

The second and third case studies testify that students improved efficiency and learned to analyse the consequences of possible actions. They preferred a long-term gain over a short-term one.

Having acquired a deeper insight into the simulation model the students made a number of suggestions about its further development. It was found reasonable to incorporate endogenous science and technology (mainly in-house R&D) into the model to reflect the relationship between science, technology and the market place.

The next step was a recognition "that, for certain kind of activities essential to technical progress, external economies and uncertainties tend to drive a wedge between private incentive and social return and for others scale requirements may dwarf the capabilities of unaided private incentives" (see Nelson, Peck and Kalachek 1967: 159). Hence there was understanding of the need for technology infrastructure and compensatory public policies to increase private incentives and capabilities.

The participants extended production by resolving incompatible norms and setting new priorities with associated strategies of co-operative behaviour. These experiments illustrate the irreversibility of economic development and show a tendency towards a higher level of (self-)organisation as shown by some indicators of efficiency and effectiveness.

The progressive evolution accelerates if gamers are provided with additional information (for example, by teaching). Social change as a result of a learning process does seem to occur in societies. J. G. Miller (1978: 860) writes: "Nations undergoing development now do not pass through all the evolutionary stages by which more advanced societies reached their present stages of development. Instead, they telescope the processes that originally took centuries into a few years of profound alteration of structure and process."

It might be reasonable to imagine that the successive experiments represent the development of two countries. The second least developed country took advantage by learning the methods of production which had been used in the first one. Therefore these experiments would appear to confirm the thesis that international learning represents the source of international gains (Pasinetti 1981).

The experiments give support to the idea of a self-organisation tendency inside a market economy but clearly not in the textbook neo-classical manner. They have shown, in particular, that a monopolised market economy could not automatically overcome a deep economic crisis and is not immune from self-destruction; irrationality or myopic rationality at a local level could produce collective irrationality if some critical positive feedback loops (vicious circles) run unchecked. I will return to this point in Chapter 6.

Costs of pre-market co-operation were not considered in the experiments. It is a task for future research to find out the consequences of taking these costs explicitly into account (especially for a number of players $N \gg 9$).[4]

Last but not least, the games started each time at the same initial conditions. Reality differs from the imaginary world on this critical point. Therefore you and I will never have a second opportunity to make a first impression on anybody, dear reader! So I will try to be smarter at the very beginning of the next chapter.

NOTES

1. A colleague of mine from the USA has gifted me a badge with an ironical phrase "Currently seeking a country to rule" after the presentation of my 1990 paper at the International System Dynamics Conference in Boston. This paper is used in this chapter.
2. The model is based on Valtukh (1987). See Valtukh and Pusep (1988). Professor Konstantin K. Valtukh and Mrs Frida Pusep have kindly provided me with their computer program. See also Ryzhenkov (1990, 1991a, b, 1993b).
3. See definition of convex cone in Nikaido (1968: 33).
4. I am thankful to Professor Oleg Arkhipoff for pointing out this restriction.

A large research agenda lies ahead of us in defining, measuring, interpreting, and understanding not only productivity growth and technology change but also how they are related to each other.

The OECD experts (OECD 1991: 133, 135)

CHAPTER 3

A MODEL OF CYCLICAL GROWTH

The hidden interplay between real wages, rate of employment and technological advance is attracting the growing attention of scientists facing the instability of the world economy. The examination of these relations is the subject for scrutiny in this and following chapters (see also Ryzhenkov 1993a,b, 1995b, 1997b, 1998b).

3.1 THE PREMISES OF THE MODEL

The model is based on Marx's methodological assumption that capitalism has its own internal regulating mechanisms. It uses his fundamental idea that economic growth, technological progress and cycles arise out of causes which are inherent in the essence of the capitalist economy. The cyclical development of the latter in turn shapes the conditions that are more or less favourable to technological innovation. Our approach is also close to Kondratiev's view on the long cycle as an expression of capitalism's internal forces. We do not share the Schumpeterian opposite view that long cycles are caused by, and are an incident of, the innovation process.

The capitalist economy at a high level of abstraction is not restricted by natural resources at first. This assumption will be relaxed in Chapter 6. The other most important premises are the following:

1. Two social classes (capitalists and workers); the state enforces property rights, yet the costs of such an enforcement are not treated explicitly.
2. Only two factors of production, labour force and means of production, both homogenous and non-specific.
3. Only one good is produced for consumption, investment and circulation purposes, its price is identically one.
4. Production (supply) equals effective demand.
5. All productive capacities are operated.
6. All wages consumed, all profits saved and invested (private consumption of capitalists and their families is not taken into account).
7. Steady growth in the labour force that is not necessarily fully employed.
8. A growth rate of a unit real wage rises in the neighbourhood of full employment.
9. A change in capital intensity and technical progress are not separable due to a flow of invention and innovation over time.

10. Total wage paid during a period of time equals capital outlay for labour power multiplied by a number of turnovers of variable capital (n_v) during this period; for simplicity n_v equals one.
11. A qualification of the labour force corresponds to technological requirements.
12. Fixed assets and labour are essentially complementary to each other and are also substitutes to some degree, depending on relative price changes. "Mechanisation is encouraged by a high wage share, i.e. high labour costs per unit of net product" (Glombowski and Krüger 1984: 265). Inflation — the other way for raising the profit share in the national income — is not treated explicitly in this model.

The model operates on the premise that the technological and institutional set-ups of society essentially determine the rates of technical progress and of capital accumulation. Technology may play an important role in monitoring the labour process and enforcement of property rights. This aspect is touched upon in the work of Bowles, Gordon and Weisskopf (1986, 1989). They consider long swings of economic activity in the context of the social structure of accumulation. The latter includes the web of laws and regulations that govern the operation of labour markets and the relationships between the capitalist class and the rest of society.

The product–money identity and the supply–demand equivalence stated in the third and fourth assumptions do not mean that we abstract from the twofold character of labour embodied in commodities entirely. This model mirrors the twofold nature of labour power, the unity and contradiction of its value and use value. The creative functions of the labour market as an instrument for transmitting impulses to economic change are the focal point of this model.

The problems of allocation of given resources and transaction costs at the micro-level are not treated explicitly. K. Marx (1978a: 598) wrote that one should not confuse "the laws that regulate the general movement of wages, or the ratio between the working class — i.e. the total labour-power — and the total social capital, with the laws that distribute the working population over the different spheres of production".

The model does not describe the formation of the real income of unemployed people. I assume that a part of wages and salaries covers indirectly the needs of the unemployed. The latter do not play an active role in the model economy. Social security contributions and benefits are not explicitly shown.

The model omits Goodwin's assumption of constant capital–output ratio, but preserves his premise of the supremacy of production over final demand. This assumption abstracts from the relative independence of final demand and changes in a product mix. It is more acceptable for the long run than for the short run: although in the shorter run aggregate demand influences output, in the very long run output dominates over demand. Capital adapts output to the scale of production.

We abstract from the overproduction of commodities inherent in the overproduction of capital during certain phases of industrial cycles. We also neglect changes in the intensity of labour. Assumption (10) not only simplifies the definition of the profit rate. It may be a key to explaining the fact that the rate of profit on capital of an order of 15 or 20% per annum is compatible with a rate of economic growth of 2 or 3% per annum (if $n_v \geq 1$).

Assumption (5) is a strongly ameliorating idealisation excluding excessive productive capacities in such forms of productive capital as machines, buildings, etc. Assumption (7) means that the labour force grows exponentially over time. This assumption may be substituted by an assumption of an asymptotic growth or another hypothesis. The growth rate of the labour force (n) depends on the rate of growth of the working age population (p) and on the participation rate of the labour force $(r) : n = p + r$. More elaborate versions of the model may take these and demographic relationships into account. We abstract from the following factors additionally: changes in the duration of the working day, the variability of overtime, involuntary retirement of the workforce.[1]

It is necessary to mention such a prominent feature of the real data as a negative correlation of population growth rates with the level of income per capita for a cross-section of countries (see Table 3.1, where Russia is a special case). On the other hand, the participation rate usually increases in a period of a growing demand for labour and decreases in a period of slackening demand (see Table 3.2). These relationships should be included in a more complex version of the model.

The supply of labour power is relatively independent of the general growth of the labour force owing to a reserve army of labour. Both supply of and demand for the labour power interact with other structural elements of capital accumulation.

Many different kinds of labour are reduced to average labour or, according to the other interpretation, they are aggregated in accordance with their informational content. An exact definition of this reduction or aggregation is not the task of the present research.

Assumptions (9) and (11) may be viewed as another simplification of reality. They presuppose very well-functioning systems of R&D, education, training and retraining of employees. To be suited for the requirements of technological progress is especially problematic for the chronically unemployed. Technology and human resource policies of the state remain beyond the confines of our model. The explicit treatment of human capital is also outside the model boundaries.

Table 3.1   Growth of population and gross domestic product

	Average growth of population (%)	Change in GDP per capita (%)
	1970–92	1970–91
World	1.7	–
Developed market economies	0.9	2.1
Developing countries[a]	2.1	1.8
Asian NIEs[b]	1.5	6.2[c]
Russia[d]	0.5	−1.0
Least developed countries	2.6	−0.7

[a] Without the socialist countries in Asia.
[b] Newly industrialised economies: Hong Kong, Singapore, Taiwan, Republic of Korea.
[c] 1972–92. *Source*: Institut der deutschen Wirtschaft Köln (1994a: 2.)
[d] 1980–93. *Source*: The World Bank (1995: 163, 211).

Table 3.2   Average annual growth of population, labour force and participation rate (%)

	Population		Labour force		Participation rate[a]	
	1970–80	1980–93	1970–80	1980–93	1970–80	1980–93
USA	1.1	1.0	2.3	1.0	1.3	0
Germany	0.1	0.2	0.6	−0.8	0.5	−1.0

[a] Author's own calculations. *Source*: The World Bank (1995: 211).

Assumption (6) corresponds to the immediate aim of capitalist production. Capital produces surplus product and profit as a monetary form of surplus value. The bounded rationality of economic behaviour and the ability of economic agents to learn are also among the premises of this post-Marxian model. With the lack of substantial empirical evidence I will not use the profit-maximising hypothesis applied by neo-classical economists.

3.2   THE MODEL EQUATIONS

The model is formulated in continuous time. Time derivatives are denoted by a dot, while growth rates are indicated by a hat. The simplified version of the model consists of the following equations:

$$P = K/s \tag{3.1}$$

$$a = P/L \tag{3.2}$$

$$u = w/a \tag{3.3}$$

$$\hat{a} = m_1 + m_2(\hat{K/L}), \quad m_1 \geq 0, 1 \geq m_2 \geq 0 \tag{3.4}$$

$$(\hat{K/L}) = n_1 + n_2 u, \quad n_2 \geq 0 \tag{3.5}$$

$$v = L/N \tag{3.6}$$

$$N = N_0 e^{nt}, \quad n = \text{const} \geq 0, N_0 > 0 \tag{3.7}$$

$$\hat{w} = -g_1 + rv, \quad g_1 \geq 0, r > 0 \tag{3.8}$$

$$M = (1 - w/a)P = (1 - u)P \tag{3.9}$$

$$\dot{K} = (1 - u)P \quad \text{or} \quad P = wL + \dot{K}. \tag{3.10}$$

Equation (3.1) postulates a technical relation between the capital stock (K) and net output (P). The variable s is called the capital–output ratio. Equation (3.2) relates labour productivity (a), net output (P) and labour input or employment (L). Equation (3.3) describes the shares of labour in national income (u). Equation (3.6) outlines the rate of employment (v) as a result of the buying and selling of labour power. Equations (3.9) and (3.10) reflect production of surplus product and its conversion into capital. They show that profit (M), savings, investment and incremental capital ($\dot{K}$) are equal. Workers do not save at all.

The next peculiarity of this model is that it has only implicit delays. Because of these, we get rid of the instantaneous adjustment to an equilibrium with full employment of the labour force used by the earlier neo-classical theories of economic growth. An explicit investment delay is still set aside. This omission is made in order to make the model simpler for analytical treatment. Introduction of a material delay in the equation for capital formation (3.10) should not be carried out in a mechanistic way. It requires modification of other parameters of the model in order to maintain its stability properties.

The importance of investment delays and lags was investigated with the help of mathematical models by M. Kalecki, S. M. Menshikov and other economists. N. F. Shatilov, M. A. Gershenzon, V. K. Ozerov, Vic. N. Pavlov, O. A. Baranov and their colleagues have developed dynamic input–output models with construction lags for middle-term projections at the Institute for Economics and Industrial Engineering (the Siberian Branch of the Russian Academy of Sciences).[2]

J. Forrester and J. Sterman consider time lags involved in investment as the essential element of an economic structure underlining the long wave. At MIT these economists have also developed effective methods of analysing growth dynamics, in which the self-ordering of equipment by the capital goods sector plays a central role.

Equation (3.10) is also the balance between the net output P and the sum of the workmen's consumption wL and net capital accumulation $\dot{K}$. The immediate effect of an increase in relative wages is depressive for investment. Still such an increase induces labour-saving technical change.

Keynes and Harrod provided the analysis of an expansion in demand resulting from increasing investment in terms of the multiplier. The ratio $1/(1-u)$ may be considered a multiplier in this model, since each additional unit of investment demand results in $1/(1-u)$ units of output. That will require $\bar{s}$ units of additional capital to produce an extra unit of output ($\bar{s}$ is a marginal capital–output ratio, $\bar{s} = \dot{K}/\dot{P}$). It follows from these premises that the actual rate of growth of output g_f equals $(1-u)/\bar{s}$. What actually happens is according to the material balance:

$$P = \dot{K} + uP = \bar{s}\dot{P} + uP,$$

hence

$$\hat{P} = \dot{P}/P = (1-u)/\bar{s} = g_f.$$

This result is derived from Harrod's use of the acceleration principle.[3] The modelling of a multiplier–accelerator mechanism helps us to find a relationship between income distribution and capital accumulation.

Unlike N. D. Kondratiev, we do not postulate that the production factors are paid according to their marginal productivity (see Kondratiev 1990: 413). His approach to economic dynamics requires

$$P = \frac{\partial P}{\partial K}K + \frac{\partial P}{\partial L}L.$$

It will be shown below that usage of such an imputation formula leads to unsatisfactory results in neo-classical models of cyclical growth. We do not use Kondratiev's hypothesis of a logistic growth of capital, population and technical level that implies a general tendency of the profit rate to fall (see Kondratiev 1990: 413).

The interesting problem remains of whether the thermodynamic laws allow exponential technical change. If efficiency improvements in cumulative energy use per unit of capital and per unit of output are bounded from above, then maximum efficiency may only be reached asymptotically. We have assumed instead that such a finite asymptote does not exist or is not of primary importance in the mean time. This issue raised by the Joule project at MERIT should be addressed in further research (see MERIT 1996: 42–43).

Technical composition of capital (K/L) and capital intensity are the same in our model. Progressive change in the technical composition of capital occurs simultaneously with the progress of accumulation. This law was stated more or less accurately by Ricardo, Sismondi and other economists.

Equation (3.4) is a linear form of Kaldor's technical progress function: the growth rate of labour productivity is assumed to depend linearly on the growth rate of capital intensity. "The use of more capital per worker ... inevitably entails the introduction of superior techniques which require 'inventiveness' of some kind .... On the other hand, most ... technical innovations which are capable of raising productivity of labour require the use of more capital per man — more elaborate equipment ..." (Kaldor 1957: 595). G. A. Feldman, a predecessor of Kaldor, studied the functional relationship between capital intensity and labour productivity in the former Soviet Union (cf. Kazantzev 1980).

The innovations should, of course, materialise in new investments. It first requires investment in capital goods industries, a process that can feed on itself for decades. Sterman (1992: 7) writes: "The process of rebuilding necessarily causes the economy to overshoot the long-run needs of replacement of depreciated assets and long-run growth." The long-term dynamics of capital goods industries, excess capacities and self-ordering of durable assets are not treated explicitly in my model of the long wave.

Kaldor recalled that the knowledge needed to increase productivity is acquired through the process of learning. It is inseparable from the process of investment, and hence the pace of applied technical progress depends on the rate of investment. The close correlation between labour productivity and capital intensity has been revealed for 13 sectors of the Austrian economy in the cross-section analysis above (see section 1.3).

Kaldor has generally been right in his criticisms of the neo-classical concept of production function that separates productivity gains due to capital accumulation from those due to technical advance. Still it is necessary to refine some elements of his approach.

Kaldor's assumption of a constant flow of invention and innovation over time, in particular, is at odds with the technical progress function with constant parameters based on an exponential growth of technological knowledge over the long term. Moreover, the flow of invention and innovation is contingent on the rate of capital accumulation. Therefore this assumption is not used in my model. Although exogenous bunching or clustering of innovations is not assumed, the model is capable of generating long waves (see Chapter 5) extraneous to the Kaldor model (1957).

Equation (3.7) defines the exponential growth of the labour supply (N) with the rate n. The employment ratio v is such that usually $0 < v < 1$. Demand for labour power does not necessarily keep pace with accumulation of capital, so the unemployment ratio $1 - v$ may grow. Absorption of the unemployed by the government sector is not modelled.

Marx (1978a: 575, 596) wrote: "... sooner or later a point must be reached, at which the requirements of accumulation begin to surpass the customary supply of labour, and, therefore, a rise of wages take place ... the general movements of wages are exclusively regulated by the expansion and contraction of the industrial reserve army, and these again correspond to the periodic changes of the industrial cycle".

The real historical experience and many empirical studies support the close positive relationship between a rate of change of a unit real wage and the employment ratio (see Jeske and Barbier 1993: 181). Involuntary unemployment is conceived by intellectuals as a massive market failure with unavoidable welfare losses (e.g. see Weitzman 1985: 403–409). This means that the mixed market economy cannot attain a state of efficiency on its own without a supportive and sophisticated public policy.

A. Phillips put the relationship between the employment ratio and growth rate of real wages in a mathematical form. Equation (3.8) represents the linear approximation of the real Phillips curve. In this equation, g_1 and r are the intercept and slope, respectively: the first reflects the tendency of capitalist production to push the value of labour power more or less to its minimum level, the second represents working men's bargaining power. A rising rate of employment is assumed to affect wage increases (in real terms). There is no money illusion. This equation will be augmented below.

Ricardo and Marx wrote that machinery is in constant competition with labour and can often be introduced when the price of labour has reached a certain height. A mechanisation function, which follows from assumption (12), is introduced in (3.5). It relates the growth rate of capital per employee (of capital intensity) to income distribution (see also Figure 3.1). The saving of social labour is not the objective aim of capitalist production and the subjective goal of a capitalist, as has been stressed in Chapter 2. Note that the mechanisation (automation) may reduce the demand for labour power if it is not counteracted.

There exists another facet of this relation. "By making labour more expensive relative to capital, [trade] unions give firms an incentive to increase the capital intensity of production. They function as a benevolent constraint ..., discouraging employers from using low-wage labour as a substitute for capital and thereby inducing technological progress", L. Kenworthy (1995: 119) writes.

Equation (3.5), written as $\hat{L} = \hat{K} - (n_1 + n_2 u)$, is in agreement with Marx's idea that "in the progress of industry the demand for labour keeps no pace with accumulation of capital" because of a progressive change in the organic composition of capital (Marx 1970: 53–54). Note that in this model the growth rates of the organic and technical composition of capital are identical and equal to $\hat{K}/L$. This equation demonstrates that demand for labour by firms depends upon the relationship between wages and productivity (the unit labour costs). It is measured by u.

The above model is different from the Menshikov–Klimenko linear model of the long wave (Menshikov and Klimenko 1985). The employment ratio and relative wage are not treated explicitly in their model. The Menshikov–Klimenko model is based on the assumption that labour productivity adjusts to capital intensity, and the latter to the profit rate, while the relative wage is considered constant. The purpose of their later study was to disaggregate capital investments into components with a specific effect on structural change. They built a model which describes the interplay between various components of investments and long waves (see Menshikov and Klimenko 1989: 145–166).

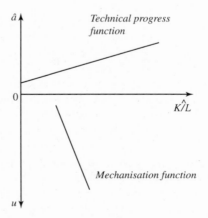

Figure 3.1   The linear approximations of the technical progress and mechanisation functions. Adapted from Glombowski and Krüger (1984: 266)

My post-Marxian approach can be compared with the neo-classical one. An article, the first of a series on economic fallacies, expresses the latter as follows: "Say firms invested less in machinery, and so productivity growth was reduced. Then unless workers also accepted smaller pay rises than before, the cost of hiring the 'marginal' worker would now exceed the value of his extra output — so unemployment would rise rather than fall ..." (*The Economist* 1995, 337 (7942): 21–22). It is possible to trace different consequences of both approaches with the help of Goodwinian models (see below).

In our model, the warranted rate of growth is equal to the profit rate:

$$g_w = \hat{K} = (1 - u)/s.$$

M. Kalecki studied a more general case in another framework. He showed that the warranted rate of growth equals $(1 - u)/\bar{s} - d + c$, where $\bar{s}$ is the incremental capital–output ratio, d the coefficient of the scrapping of old capacities and c the coefficient of improvement in utilisation of productive capacity. The notion of warranted rate of growth is associated with the work done by R. F. Harrod and E. D. Domar in the 1930s and 1940s.

The natural rate of growth is the sum of labour supply growth and productivity growth:

$$g_n = \hat{a} + n.$$

The actual rate of growth is the difference between the profit rate and the rate of growth of the capital–output ratio:

$$g_f = \hat{P} = \hat{K} - \hat{s} = (1 - u)/s - \hat{s}.$$

The model provides us with a possibility of investigating an adjustment mechanism between g_w, g_n and g_f working through the share of profit in income and capital intensity. Another model could be built if assumption (12) was substituted by a hypothesis of a constant capital–output ratio and exogenously given rate of technological progress:

$$\hat{a} = m_1 + m_2(\hat{K/L}) = m_1 + m_2\hat{a}, \tag{3.11}$$

where $m_1 > 0$, $1 > m_2 > 0$, hence

$$\hat{a} = m_1/(1 - m_2).$$

This model does not possess the mechanisation function but retains the other assumptions and equations. Still it is not a special case of the first model that could be derived by simply postulating that $n_1 = n_2 = 0$. It presupposes capital intensity is growing in the long run because of conversion of profit into capital. Investment behaviour is too rigid as the capital–output ratio remains constant.

The initial system (3.1)–(3.10) has *a full employment stationary state* without technical change and factor substitution. In this case, the initial share of workers in net output equals one ($u_0 = 1$) and the following requirements are satisfied:

$$v_0 = g_1/r = 1, \quad s_0 = K_0/P_0 > 0, \quad n = 0, \quad n_1 = -n_2, \quad m_1 = 0, 1 \geq m_2 \geq 0.$$

Then

$$u = u_0 = 1, \quad v = v_0 = 1, \quad s = s_0.$$

Surplus product and profit are not produced in this stationary state. Neglecting the private consumption of capitalists allows us to consider the full employment stationary state of the system (3.1)–(3.10) as simple reproduction. In reality, capitalist production requires $u < 1$ and $v < 1$. The additional requirements will be imposed below for an extended version of this model.

3.3 IMPLICATIONS OF VALTUKH'S INFORMATION VALUE HYPOTHESIS

The wealth of nations and their competitive advantages are crucially dependent on a highly trained labour force. The shift towards ever more capital-intensive production makes skilled labour increasingly scarce relative to demand in the industrialised market economies.

In his influential book *The Work of Nations* Robert Reich calls for a national recommitment to the productivity and competitiveness of *all* nations' citizens. It is the skills and capacities of the people that have become the primary assets, and that must become the focus of social scientists' attention. "The skills of a nation's work force and the quality of its infrastructure are what makes it unique and uniquely attractive in the world economy" (Reich 1991: 264). The complexity of modern technology and the large size of firms require firm-specific on-the-job training, internal promotion ladders and a stable and loyal workforce.

It is well known that Karl Marx left unsolved the problem of reduction of qualified labour to simple labour in his theory of commodity and surplus value. The Valtukh information value hypothesis is an attempt to generalise the labour theory of value and free it from internal contradictions. According to it, the value of labour power of a particularly large qualification group (p_θ, $\theta \in \Theta$, Θ is a set of qualification groups in the economy) and the amount of its direct labour (l_θ) are connected by the following relationship (in statics) (see Valtukh 1991: 21–44):

$$p_\theta = \alpha_\theta \psi_\theta l_\theta, \tag{3.12}$$

where Ψ_θ is the coefficient of reduction of qualified labour to simple labour, α_θ is the distributive share of the qualification group in value added by this group,

$$\alpha_\theta > 0, \quad \forall \theta \in \Theta,$$

$$\alpha_\theta = f(\psi_\theta), \quad \mathrm{d}\alpha_\theta/\mathrm{d}\psi_\theta < 0, \quad \text{and} \quad \mathrm{d}p_\theta/\mathrm{d}\psi_\theta > 0.$$

The hypothesis evinces that the rate of surplus value, all other things being equal, grows along with qualification (see a snapshot in Figure 3.2).

The technical qualification of the workforce depends upon the availability of fixed assets (first of all equipment) on which to learn and gain experience. The higher the qualification, the higher the capital intensity, and vice versa. In my opinion, the capital intensity may be used as the indicator of qualification in dynamics as well. This conjecture will help us to extend the model of capital accumulation.

Instead of assuming, as in the usual Phillips relation, that the rate of change of the wage rate (w) depends only on the employment rate (v), let this rate be additionally influenced by the rate of change of capital intensity (K/L):

$$\hat{w} = -g_1 + rv + g_2 + b(\widehat{K/L}), \tag{3.13}$$

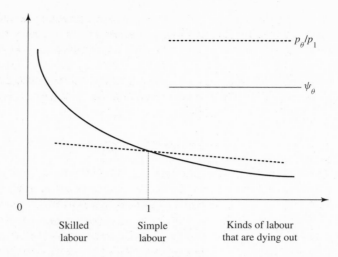

Figure 3.2   Coefficients of reduction of skilled labour to simple labour (ψ_θ) and ratios of wage rates (p_θ/p_1) for different qualification groups ($\theta \in \Theta$), the group of simple labour has the index 1

where $g_2 \geq 0$, $b > 0$. It is assumed in addition that the static relationship between the rate of surplus value and qualification is valid for the system dynamics as well, so $b < m_2$.

This modification also takes into consideration the historical or moral element in the value of labour power. It may be helpful in explaining the downward rigidity of the real wage. Equation (3.13) will be used in obtaining a convenient statement of the model. It will be shown below that the proposed modification of the usual Phillips relation has far-reaching consequences for the system behaviour.

The diffusion of lean production in the industrialised countries based on re-engineering, training employees in multiple skills and pushing decision-making authority as far down in an organisation as possible, empirically supports these arguments (see Ehrbar and Roth 1993). Furthermore, this upgrading tendency obviously outweighs a counter-tendency. The latter may prevail in some branches or even in an economy as a whole at some periods of historical development (then $b < 0$). Please note that I am abstracting from the institutional arrangements for the supply of skills and segmentation of the labour market.

Table 3.3 contains the measurement units for the model variables and parameters. The rate of flow of current production is measured in bits of embodied information a year. Its unit price is identically one.

Labour expended on production of commodities is measured in time units (years) per year, therefore the labour resource input, L, is a number without a specific unit of measurement (dimensionless for brevity)! The labour productivity, a, and unit real wage rate, w, are measured in bits per year consequently. The reader will notice the difference between these more accurate units of measurement and those applied in Chapter 1.

Labour expended on production of commodities can also be measured in information units per year. In this case, I believe, the reader is already well prepared to modify easily the units given in Table 3.3 and obtain new ones even more different from those used in ordinary language (for example, labour productivity and unit real wage are dimensionless conversion factors).

Table 3.3 The measurement units for the variables and parameters of the cyclical growth model

Bit	Bit/year	Bit/(year^2)
K	P	$\dot{a}$
K/L	M	$\dot{w}$
	$\dot{K}$	$\dot{P}$
	$\dot{K}/L$	
	w	
	a	

Non-dimensional	1/year	Year
L	$\dot{L}$	s
N	$\dot{N}$	T
b	m_1	$\bar{s}$
m_2	$\dot{u}$	
u	$\hat{u}$	
v	$\dot{v}$	
$\dot{s}$	$\hat{v}$	
$K/(wL/n_v)$	n	
	g	
	r	
	n_1	
	n_2	
	$\hat{P}$	
	$\hat{K}$	
	$\hat{L}$	
	$\hat{K}/L$	
	$\hat{s}$	
	$\tilde{w}$	
	$\hat{a}$	
	$\hat{w}$	

3.4   THE HYPOTHETICAL LAW OF MOTION

The central variables of the modified model are the employment rate (v), the labour bill share (u) and the capital coefficient (s). To be economically meaningful, they should be strictly positive. Moreover, the rates of growth are not defined for (0, 0, 0).

Let us first consider the evolution of the capital–output ratio. Substitution and logarithmic differentiation yield

$$\hat{s} = (\hat{K/P}) = (\hat{K/L}) - (\hat{P/L}) = -m_1 - m_2(\hat{K/L}) + (\hat{K/L})$$

$$= -m_1 + (1 - m_2)(n_1 + n_2 u). \tag{3.14}$$

The employment rate (v) is defined by the equation:

$$\hat{v} = (\hat{L/N}) = \hat{P} - \hat{a} - \hat{N} = (\hat{P/K}) + \hat{K} - \hat{a} - \hat{N}$$

$$= -\hat{s} + (1 - w/a)/s - \hat{a} - n. \tag{3.15}$$

We have used in (3.15) $\hat{K} = (1 - w/a)P/K = (1 - w/a)/s$. Marx (1970: 53) was thus right arguing that "with the development of the productive powers of labour the accumulation of capital will be accelerated, even despite a relative high rate of wage".

Substitution and transformation allow us to write (3.15) in another form:

$$\hat{v} = (1 - u)/s - \hat{s} - (\hat{a} + n) = g_w - \hat{s} - g_n = g_f - g_n$$

$$= (1 - u)/s - (n_1 + n_2 u) - n. \tag{3.16}$$

Note that the difference between the actual (g_f) and natural (g_n) growth rates determines the evolution of the employment ratio in this model. "The demand for labour is not identical with increase of capital, nor supply of labour with increase of working-class. Capital works on both sides at the same time" (Marx 1978a: 599).

A growth of the economy ($g_f > n > 0$) is necessary to prevent growth of the unemployment ratio (if $\hat{a} > 0$). The further increase of g_f *may* promote the employment ratio. These conclusions are in agreement with the Okun (1962) law that explains unemployment by co-movement in output only.[4]

The rates $\hat{P}_{min}$ and $\hat{P}_{max}$ are in a one-to-one relationship with an average employment ratio in the long wave. Each other $\hat{P}(\hat{P}_{min} < \hat{P} < \hat{P}_{max})$ relates to two different ratios of employment (relatively high and low, correspondingly). On the other hand, two different rates of economic growth typically correspond with a specific employment ratio. The wave-pattern of growth explains why an increase of $\hat{P}$ fosters a greater unemployment in relative and absolute terms during a depression and promotes employment during a recovery of Kondratiev's cycle (see Figure 3.3).

An increase of g_f above some critical magnitude can result in a decrease in the rate of employment if productivity of labour ($\hat{a}$) grows sufficiently fast. This peculiarity is not clearly reflected by the Okun law.

The other possible presentation of $\hat{v}$ is the following:

$$\hat{v} = (1 - u)/s - \hat{s} - (\hat{a} + n)$$

$$= (1 - u)/s - \hat{s} - m_1 - m_2(\hat{K/L}) - n$$

$$= (1 - u)/s - \hat{s} - m_1 - m_2(1 - u)/s + m_2(\hat{v} + n) - n$$

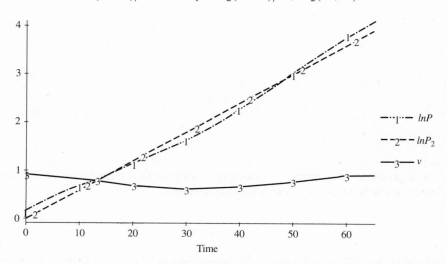

Figure 3.3   Synchronous fluctuations of the employment ratio (v) and net output ($ln\,P$) around the trend ($ln\,P_2$). P_2 grows exponentially (see formula (4.1)) and corresponds to the steady state $E_2 = (s_2, v_2, u_2)$ (3.24). Initial data are given in Table 5.3 (the non-degenerative case)

$$= (1 - u)/s - \hat{s}/(1 - m_2) - n - m_1/(1 - m_2)$$
$$= (1 - u)/s - \hat{s}/(1 - m_2) - n - \tilde{w}, \tag{3.17}$$

where $\tilde{w} = m_1/(1 - m_2)$. Hence the growth rate of the employment ratio depends on profitability and the rate of change of the capital–output ratio.

Van der Ploeg (1983: 237–239) and Zhang (1988: 162) have derived a similar expression for the rate of growth of the employment ratio in a predator–prey description of a perpetual class conflict (equations (1) and (5) in the notation of these authors, respectively).

The labour bill share (u) changes in accordance with

$$\hat{u} = (w\hat{/}a) = \hat{w} - \hat{a}$$
$$= -g + rv + b(n_1 + n_2 u) - (m_1 + m_2(n_1 + n_2 u))$$
$$= -g + rv - m_1 + (b - m_2)(n_1 + n_2 u), \tag{3.18}$$

where $g = g_1 - g_2$.

Rewriting equation (3.18) in terms of equation (3.14) we obtain an alternative equation for the labour bill share:

$$\hat{u} = -g + rv - m_1 + (b - m_2)(\hat{s}/(1 - m_2) + \tilde{w}). \tag{3.19}$$

For $b = 0$,

$$\hat{u} = -g + rv - m_2\hat{s}/(1 - m_2) - \tilde{w}. \tag{3.20}$$

Equation (3.19) may be viewed as a generalisation of the known equation for the relative wage for $b \geq 0$.[5]

The hypothetical law of motion of the model economy is given by the following system of nonlinear ordinary differential equations:

$$\dot{s} = -(m_1 + (m_2 - 1)(n_1 + n_2 u))s \tag{3.21}$$

$$\dot{v} = ((1 - u)/s - (n_1 + n_2 u) - n)v \tag{3.22}$$

$$\dot{u} = (-g + rv - m_1 + (b - m_2)(n_1 + n_2 u))u. \tag{3.23}$$

Distinct scenarios of evolution are possible, depending on the initial state and values of the parameters. It will be demonstrated below that this law of motion can drive the system towards quite different results. This conclusion would be retained if random fluctuations were incorporated in a more realistic stochastic model.

Note that equation (3.23) for the derivative of the "predator" u contains the element of a stabilising "intra-specific" competition $(b - m_2)n_2 u^2$ (for $b < m_2$). It is absent in the original predator–prey model of Goodwin. A cybernetic interpretation of this and the other equations will be given in the following sections.

3.5   THE STEADY STATE

We will use at first the simplest notion of equilibrium (a fixed point in a phase space). A non-trivial equilibrium for $m_2 \neq 1$, $n_2 > 0$ is given by

$$E_2 = (s_2, v_2, u_2), \tag{3.24}$$

where

$$u_2 = m_1/(n_2(1 - m_2)) - n_1/n_2 = (\tilde{w} - n_1)/n_2,$$

$$s_2 = (1 - u_2)/(n_1 + n_2 u_2 + n)$$

$$= (1 - u_2)/(\tilde{w} + n) = (n_1 + n_2 - \tilde{w})/(n_2(\tilde{w} + n))$$

and

$$v_2 = (g + m_1 + (m_2 - b)(n_1 + n_2 u_2))/r$$

$$= (g + m_1 + (m_2 - b)\tilde{w})/r,$$

$$= (g + (1 - b)\tilde{w})/r$$

where $\tilde{w} = n_1 + n_2 u_2 = m_1/(1 - m_2)$. It will be shown below that $\tilde{w}$ equals an equilibrium growth rate of labour productivity. (s_2 follows from (3.22), v_2 from (3.23) and u_2 from (3.21).)

It follows from (3.10) that $\hat{K} = (1 - u)P/K$ and hence

$$(K\hat{/}L) = (1 - u)P/K - \hat{L} \quad \text{or} \quad K/L = (1 - u)a - \hat{L}(K/L).$$

This equation generalises *the fundamental equation of neo-classical economic growth* corresponding to equation (6) of Solow's (1956) original paper:

$$K/L = (1 - u)a - n(K/L),$$

where $(1 - u)$ is the saving ratio.

The reader will see that the growth rate of the labour force is equal to the growth rate of employment in neo-classical growth theory, but these rates usually differ in our model. They are equal at the steady state, in particular. Unlike neo-classical Golden Ages, there is a persistent unemployment at the steady state in our model that is more realistic.

The elasticity of substitution measures *the responsiveness* of the capital intensity to the ratio of profit rate to unit real wage. We define it quite independently of impractical marginal products as

$$\sigma = -\frac{K\hat{/}L}{\hat{K}\hat{/}w} = -\frac{K\hat{/}L}{\hat{K} - \hat{w}} = -\frac{K\hat{/}L}{-\dfrac{\dot{u}}{1 - u} - \hat{s} - \hat{w}} = -\frac{K\hat{/}L}{-\dfrac{\dot{u}}{1 - u} - \hat{s} - \hat{u} - \hat{a}}$$

$$= -\frac{K\hat{/}L}{-\dfrac{\dot{u}}{1 - u} - \hat{u} - K\hat{/}L} = \frac{K\hat{/}L}{\dfrac{\hat{u}}{1 - u} + K\hat{/}L} = \frac{n_1 + n_2 u}{\dfrac{\hat{u}}{1 - u} + n_1 + n_2 u}.$$

The equilibrium marginal rate of substitution $\sigma_2 = 1$.

A positive rate of growth of output per head and stable growth can be assured even if the growth of the labour force (n) exceeds the autonomous productivity growth (m_1). This is essentially because we do not postulate full employment at the equilibrium as does Kaldor's model (1957). An increase in workers' bargaining power (r) depresses the equilibrium employment ratio (v_2), producing no influence on the equilibrium relative wage (u_2). Note

$$1 \geq u_2 > 0 \quad \text{and} \quad s_2 > 0 \quad \text{if} \quad n_1 + n_2 \geq \tilde{w} > n_1;$$

$$1 \geq v_2 > 0 \quad \text{if} \quad g + m_1 > (b - m_2)\tilde{w}$$

and

$$r \geq g + m_1 + (m_2 - b)\tilde{w} > 0.$$

The differential equation (3.21) may be written in an equivalent form:

$$\dot{s} = n_2(1 - m_2)(u - u_2)s$$
$$= n_2(1 - m_2)u_2(u/u_2 - 1)s$$
$$= (m_1 - n_1(1 - m_2))(u/u_2 - 1)s, \qquad (3.25)$$

where $0 < m_2 < 1$ and $u_2 \neq 0$, $m_1 n_1 \neq 0$ and

$$n_1 < m_1/(1 - m_2) = \tilde{w}.$$

Equation (3.25) hints at a proportional control over the capital–output ratio. At the long wave, the capital–output ratio and the labour bill share cannot equal the equilibrium magnitudes simultaneously: $u = u_2 \Leftrightarrow s_{max}$ or s_{min}, $s = s_2 \Leftrightarrow u_{max}$ or u_{min}.

By writing $\hat{K} = \hat{P} + \hat{s} = \hat{P} + n_2(1 - m_2)(u - u_2)$, we can name the determinants of investment growth relatively to existing fixed assets: a growth rate of production and demand ($\hat{P}$), an excess share of labour in national income ($u - u_2$) and the slopes of the technical progress and mechanisation functions (n_2, m_2).

The coefficients m_2 and n_2 are mostly important for a compromise between a speedy response and stability in our model economy (hence a trade-off between a period of a cycle and stability). The equilibrium labour bill share u_2 and capital–output ratio s_2 depend upon the compound coefficient $n_2(1 - m_2)$.

This very important interconnection is absent in the modern neo-classical model of cyclical growth that contains the Kaldorian technical progress function. This neo-classical model could also be represented by a system of three ordinary differential equations with nonlinearity and implicit delays. The neo-classical model uses a hypothesis that capitalists recruit labour and scrap machinery until the marginal productivity of labour ($\partial P/\partial L$) equals the real wage (w), so the equation for the capital–output ratio becomes (in my notations for the convenience of the reader):

$$\dot{s} = \xi \left[\left(\frac{u}{1 - m_2} \right)^{(1 - m_2)/m_2} - 1 \right] s,$$

where ξ is the exogenous speed of adjustment of the capital–output ratio to its equilibrium, $\xi \geq 0$; the magnitude $(1 - m_2)$ is the equilibrium relative wage (see Zhang 1988: 162–163). Parameters ξ and m_2 are postulated to be independent in this neo-classical model, although this conjecture is not justified. I will return to this neo-classical model in section 4.4.

In conclusion to this section, it is reasonable to rewrite (3.19) in terms of equations (3.24) and (3.25):

$$\hat{u} = r(v - v_2) + (b - m_2)n_2(u - u_2) = r(v - v_2) + (b - m_2)\hat{s}/(1 - m_2). \qquad (3.19')$$

It contains the elements of proportional and derivative control, $r(v - v_2)$ and $(b - m_2)\hat{s}/(1 - m_2)$, respectively. The derivative correction element $(b - m_2)\hat{s}/(1 - m_2)$ does not shift the equilibrium position. Here the derivative control produces the same effect as the "intra-specific" competition mentioned earlier.

Similarly, the presence of $\hat{s}$ in equation (3.17) for $\hat{v}$ on the right-hand side, reflecting the derivative control, does not affect the equilibrium position.

3.6 THE NECESSARY AND SUFFICIENT CONDITIONS FOR A LOCAL STABILITY

Returning to (3.17), using (3.25) for $\hat{s}$ and the equality $(1 - u)/s = \hat{K} = \hat{P} + \hat{s}$, we obtain three equations for a growth rate of the demand for employment after a simple transformation:

$$\hat{L} = \hat{v} + n$$

$$= \hat{P} + \hat{s} - \hat{s}/(1 - m_2) - \tilde{w} \tag{3.26}$$

$$= \hat{P} - \hat{s}\, m_2/(1 - m_2) - \tilde{w} \tag{3.27}$$

$$= \hat{P} - m_2 n_2 (u - u_2) - \tilde{w}. \tag{3.28}$$

These equations reveal the positive influence of growing demand on employment. It shows that the labour-reabsorbing effects of technological change do not necessarily compensate for its displacement effects. Workers are dismissed when the labour bill share in national income is higher than the equilibrium one, demand for commodities is diminishing or is growing too slowly ($\tilde{w}$ is constant here). Otherwise additional workers are hired.

Okun has shown that the workforce adjusts to oscillations in output with a time delay. Employment protection rules, employers' preference to preserve the core professionals, save transaction and training costs and other factors matter. As a result of these and other factors a substantial part of employers' outlays for the employed labour force has a fixed-cost nature (see Okun 1983). So it would be interesting to include a time delay in the dependence of $\hat{v}$ upon $\hat{a}$ and trace the consequences of labour hoarding for the system dynamics. Besides this delay, other labour market rigidities may also play an important role.

Our assumption of labour force homogeneity also restricts pragmatic interest in that equation. It is necessary to pay attention to changes in the skill structure of the labour force and its distribution between the different sectors of the economy.

The skills of dismissed labourers seeking admission may not match those needed by the firms looking for labourers. The qualification of chronically unemployed people may deteriorate to such an extent that they will be excluded from the labour market. However, these peculiarities are mostly extraneous for our abstract and idealised capitalist economy.

"Given the market failure in human capital and in job matching, government assistance can improve labour market performance", L. Kenworthy (1995: 92) writes. I believe that the problems of *structural unemployment* could be investigated with the help of dynamic input–output models of the (inter-)national economy.

Equation (3.22) for $\hat{v}$ is not analytical for $s = 0$. If we introduce a variable for the output–capital ratio, $z = 1/s$, instead of s, the system (3.21)–(3.23) is transformed into an equivalent form:

$$\dot{z} = -n_2(1 - m_2)(u - u_2)z \tag{3.29}$$

$$\dot{v} = ((1 - u)z - (n_1 + n_2 u) - n)v \tag{3.30}$$

$$\dot{u} = (-g + rv - m_1 + (b - m_2)(n_1 + n_2 u))u. \tag{3.31}$$

Equations (3.23) and (3.31) are identical. This system has the trivial fixed point equilibrium $(0, 0, 0)$ in addition to the non-trivial one (z_2, v_2, u_2), where $z_2 = 1/s_2$. However, this point must be excluded from the acceptable quantity range as the rates of growth of the model variables $(\hat{K}/L$ and others) cannot be defined for $(0, 0, 0)$.

The three-dimensional system (3.21)–(3.23) is obviously nonlinear and could, potentially, display a very rich spectrum of behaviour. Closed-form analytical solutions are not available. It contains nonlinearity of a higher order than the renowned Lorenz model of fluid convection.

If $m_1 = 0$ and $m_2 = 1$, then $\dot{s} = 0$ and the initial condition $(s = s_0 > 0)$ determines the constant capital–output ratio. The system degenerates into the two-dimensional system:

$$\dot{v} = ((1 - u)/s_0 - (n_1 + n_2u) - n)v \tag{3.32}$$

$$\dot{u} = (-g + rv + (b - 1)(n_1 + n_2u))u. \tag{3.33}$$

The non-trivial equilibrium in this case is given by

$$u_e = (1 - s_0(n_1 + n))/(n_2s_0 + 1),$$

$$v_e = (g + (1 - b)(n_1 + n_2u_e))/r. \tag{3.34}$$

We will provide an example of a long wave for this case in section 5.1. The reader may notice that the famous Goodwin model (1972) is a special case of this model for $n_1 > 0$, $n_2 = 0$, $b = 0$.

The Jacobian of the three-dimensional system evaluated at the non-trivial equilibrium E_2 is given by

$$J = \begin{vmatrix} 0 & 0 & n_2(1 - m_2)s_2 \\ -v_2(1 - u_2)/s_2^2 & 0 & -v_2/s_2 - n_2v_2 \\ 0 & ru_2 & (b - m_2)n_2u_2 \end{vmatrix}. \tag{3.35}$$

Thus, the characteristic polynomial is $\lambda^3 + a_2\lambda^2 + a_1\lambda + a_0 = 0$, where

$$a_0 = -\det(J) = (v_2(1 - u_2)ru_2n_2(1 - m_2))/s_2 > 0, \quad \text{if} \quad m_2 < 1 \text{ and } n_2 > 0;$$

$$a_1 = ru_2v_2(1/s_2 + n_2) > 0;$$

$$a_2 = -\text{trace}(J) = (m_2 - b)n_2u_2 > 0, \quad \text{if} \quad m_2 > b. \tag{3.36}$$

The Routh–Hourwitz conditions are necessary and sufficient for local stability and require that $a_0 > 0$, $a_1 > 0$ and $a_1a_2 > a_0$. The first and second inequalities are satisfied, whereas the third inequality corresponds to

$$(n_2s_2 + 1)(m_2 - b) > ((1 - u_2)/u_2)(1 - m_2) > 0. \tag{3.37}$$

Provided that the inequality (3.37) holds, the dynamics of the modified model (3.21)–(3.23), in the neighbourhood of its equilibrium, are Poincaré (locally) stable (cf. van der Ploeg 1987). Then the eigenvalues have negative real parts. The inequality (3.37) is not true if $m_2 \leq b$. So $m_2 > b$ is a necessary condition of the local stability. Note that in (3.37) $(1 - u_2)/u_2$ is equal to the rate of surplus value estimated at the equilibrium.

The stationary state solution without surplus product, $u = u_0 = 1$, $v = v_0 = 1$, $s = s_0$, is not stable in the three-dimensional system. Surplus product is a *conditio sine qua non* for growth and stability of the capitalist economy.

Equation (3.17) helps us to understand better the balancing and enforcing feedback mechanisms inherent in the model economy. At $u = 1$ profit evaporates. So it is a matter of utmost concern how close u is to 1. If production is so close as to become unprofitable, entrepreneurs will be more eager to force down employment. The component $(1 - u)$ has a structural similarity with the deviation $(u_2 - u)$. In my opinion, it may be interpreted as the element of proportional control. The number 1 is the supremum of the relative wage in a capitalist economy, from the economic point of view. Usage of the supremum magnitude (1) along with u_2 in the feedback mechanisms allows extended reproduction of the model economy.

Unlike previous modes of production with their conservative technological base, industrial capitalism is characterised by evolutionary and revolutionary technological transformations based on a systematic and wide-scale usage of theoretical and applied knowledge (mostly natural sciences). On the one hand, technological progress disturbs market equilibrium; on the other, it exerts a stabilising influence on economic dynamics and income distribution. The presence of the coefficient $n_2 > 0$ on the left-hand side of (3.37) shows that. Still one should also keep in mind the possibility of a destabilising influence if this coefficient exceeds some critical value. Too aggressive an increase in the speed of distribution-induced technological progress may be detrimental for the system stability (see below).

At the conclusion of this section, let us compare properties of the basic model, described by (3.21)–(3.23), and the simpler model, given by (3.1)–(3.4) and (3.6)–(3.11). The higher the equilibrium rate of productivity growth ($\bar{w}$), the higher the employment ratios (v_2 and v_3, if $b < 1$). In the latter model, increases in the rate of technical progress ($\bar{w}$) and in the rate of growth of the labour force (n) depress the equilibrium relative wage (u_3)[6]. In the former, an increase in the growth rate of the labour force produces no effect on the equilibrium relative wage (u_2). Paradoxically, faster technical progress promotes the equilibrium relative wage (u_2).

Thus distribution-induced technical progress brings about a qualitative change in the pattern of evolution. In particular, it changes stability properties of the model. The simpler model may be considered a historical predecessor of our basic model with a greater number of causal connections.

The regulation progresses through changing the basic relations. Capitalists and workers learn from experience (and social sciences, perhaps) that the lack of investment flexibility is detrimental for capital accumulation and well-being. They invent new behavioural algorithms that raise the organisational complexity and improve economic efficiency. Such changes in production relations are based on and supported by technological advance. Yet the new stabilisation mechanism inevitably brings about additional sources of instability that can dominate under certain conditions. External perturbations could also challenge the resilience of the system. The more so, as "the threat of disruption is always present in a dynamic market economy" (*Economic Report of the President* 1999: 20). I incline to agree with M. Pugno (1989: 256) that "the research on growth as a stable process where instability episodes are exceptional should be switched to research on growth as an unstable process, because instability episodes are its necessary premise and outcome".

NOTES

1. See an excellent treatment of this subject in Biffl (1994).
2. See, for instance, one of the recent publications on this subject, Baranov and Pavlov (1994).
3. Different hypotheses concerning magnitudes of multiplier and accelerator are presented in Granberg (1985: 45–55).
4. Reprinted in Okun (1983). See about this empirical law also in Fischer, Dornbusch and Schmalensee (1988: Chapter 32) and in *Economic Report of the President* (1999: 83).
5. This expression has a close correspondence with formula (2″) in van der Ploeg (1983: 246) and formula (10) in Zhang (1988: 163).
6. $u_3 = 1 - (\tilde{w} + n)s_0, v_3 = (g + \tilde{w})/r$.

The most striking fact ... is that the
share of labour [in net national product] is
higher, the higher the growth rate. This may in
part be due to the particular choice of
parameters, but it does indicate that such a
result is possible.

Richard M. Goodwin (1990: 79)

CHAPTER 4

CAPITAL ACCUMULATION AS A COMPETITIVE–CO-OPERATIVE SYSTEM

This chapter focuses on issues of stability, fluctuations and long-run trends in relation to improving skills and growing capital intensity. It reveals pitfalls of involuntary learning and illustrates gains in efficiency due to voluntary learning. Uncovering fundamental regulating mechanisms inherent in the capitalist economy helps to design policies needed nowadays for sustainable development.

4.1   THE TREND IN THE MODELLING ECONOMY

We abstract from short-term business cycles and from the 15- to 25-year construction cycles, which have been identified by economists in macroeconomic systems. We disregard random noise, which manifests itself in arbitrary variations in the growth rate in the short run.

The average growth rate of the real per capita GDP in the USA during 1870–1990 was 1.75% per annum. The real GDP grew in this period from \$2224 to \$18 258 per capita (1985 dollars). If the average growth rate was 0.75% per annum, the real GDP would be \$5519 per capita in 1990, i.e. at the level that is closer to Mexico's (see *Business Week* 1996, No. 1: 9).

Over the very long time span, technical progress and the growth of the labour force result in steady economic growth — about 3.4% a year since 1880 in the USA (see Sterman 1992: 4). Extended reproduction along the steady-state path in the model displays such an exponential growth. Output expands at its natural rate (g_n) that is equal to the warranted rate of growth (g_w):

$$\hat{P}_2 = \hat{a}_2 + n = m_1/(1 - m_2) + n \qquad (4.1)$$

$$= \tilde{w} + n = (1 - u_2)/s_2. \qquad (4.2)$$

The growth of capital intensity (organic and technical composition of capital), labour productivity and real wage is at the rate

$$\hat{K_2/L_2} = n_1 + n_2 u_2 = \hat{a}_2 = \hat{w}_2 = m_1/(1 - m_2) = \tilde{w}, \qquad (4.3)$$

if $m_1 \neq 0$ and $m_2 \neq 1$, or at the rate

$$K_e\hat{/}L_e = \hat{a}_e = \hat{w}_e = n_1 + n_2 u_e, \qquad (4.4)$$

if $m_1 = 0$ and $m_2 = 1$ (see (3.34) above).

At the same time the profit share, the capital–output ratio and, therefore, the rate of profit itself are constant. Capital stock increases at the rate

$$\hat{K}_2 = \hat{P}_2 \qquad (4.5)$$

which is equal to the profit rate

$$M_2/K_2 = \hat{K}_2 = \hat{P}_2. \qquad (4.6)$$

In the degenerate case we have

$$M_e/K_e = \hat{K}_e = \hat{P}_e. \qquad (4.7)$$

The equilibrium profit rate is the reciprocal of the product of the acceleration and multiplier coefficients, $[s_2/(1 - u_2)]^{-1}$ and $[s_0/(1 - u_e)]^{-1}$, respectively. The incremental and average capital–output ratios ($\bar{s}$ and s) are identical at the steady state.

The present model does not support Marx's (1978a: 566) view that real wages never rise proportionally to the productive power of labour. Continuously rising productivity is a necessary condition for a rising standard of living that fosters productivity even further. A failure to innovate is detrimental to employment, real wages and profitability, whereas increasing technical dynamism is favourable for them.

Marx, who expected the general rate of profit to fall over the long term, did not foresee the constancy of the equilibrium profit rate. He wrote (Marx 1978c: 242): "We have seen that while s, the total amount of surplus value, is continually increasing in the course of capitalist development, s/C is just as steadily declining, because C [the total social capital] grows still more rapidly than s." In our model, the profit rate decreases during the boom and recession of the long wave. It increases during the depression and recovery.

The upswing and downswing phases of the long cycle are determined relative to the steady state for relative quantities and in relation to the net output trend. The upswing consists of recovery and prosperity, the downswing embraces recession and depression. These periods are delineated based on movements of the employment ratio that mirror very closely fluctuations of net output around the trend (see Chapter 5 for more details).

The labour income share, the rate of employment and capital–output ratio are constant at the steady state. The constancy of the labour share over the long period is known as Bowley's law. This regularity is an *ex post* outcome of a succession of periods of diverging from constancy and periods that correct this divergence.

The forms of feedback control, used in the model economy, are not sufficient to eliminate deviations from the steady state and tend to cause cyclical fluctuations. However, stabilisation is not the only purpose of the control. Another is to extend the scale of production. The presence of different kinds of cycles, noise and perturbations makes the control problem harder in real life.

The value composition of capital is constant and equals the rate of surplus value divided by the growth rate of the economy (for simplicity, $n_v = 1$):

$$K_2/(w_2 L_2/n_v) = K_2/u_2 P_2 = s_2/u_2 \qquad (4.8)$$

$$= (1 - u_2)/(u_2(n_1 + n_2 u_2 + n)) \qquad (4.9)$$

$$= (1 - u_2)/(u_2(\tilde{w} + n)) = [(1 - u_2)/u_2]/(\tilde{w} + n)$$
$$= (n_1 + n_2 - \tilde{w})/[(\tilde{w} - n_1)(\tilde{w} + n)]. \tag{4.10}$$

The properties of the steady-state growth in our model are in good agreement with Kaldor's five stylised facts:

1. The aggregate volume of production and output per worker show continuing growth at a steady rate with no tendency for a falling rate of growth of productivity.
2. Capital per worker shows continuing growth.
3. The rate of profit on capital is steady at least in the developed capitalist societies.
4. The capital–output ratio is steady over long periods, hence the aggregate volume of production and fixed capital tend to grow at the same rate.
5. Labour and capital receive constant shares of total income. The shares of profit in national income and the share of investment in net output are closely (positively) correlated.

Based on historical data that characterise the process of economic growth in advanced economies, P. Romer (1989) has reproduced Kaldor's stylised facts. N. Kaldor has stressed that none of these stylised facts can be plausibly "explained" by the theoretical constructions of neo-classical theory known in his time. He has written, in particular (Kaldor 1965: 179):

> On the basis of the marginal productivity theory, and the capital theory of Böhm-Bawerk and followers, one would expect a continuing *fall* in the rate of profit with capital accumulation, and not a steady rate of profit. (In this respect classical and neo-classical theory, arguing on different grounds, come to the same conclusion — Adam Smith, Ricardo, Marx, alike with Böhm-Bawerk and Wicksell, predicted a steady fall in the rate of profit with economic progress.) Similarly, on the basis of the neo-classical approach, one expects diminishing returns to capital accumulation which implies a steady *rise* in the capital–output ratio *pari passu* with the rise in the capital–labour ratio; and a diminishing rate of growth in the productivity of labour at any given ratio of investment to output (or savings to income).

This critique has stimulated a rethinking of traditional neo-classical and Marxian postulates and a search for more powerful instruments of economic analysis. In particular, new growth theories of a neo-classical flavour "emphasise the role of economy-wide returns to scale, expenditures on R&D, human capital formation, and the mediating role of investment in the diffusion and promotion of technical change" (OECD 1992: 172).

Similar to Kaldor (1957), in our model, the form that increasing returns normally takes is that the productivity of labour rises with the scale of production, while that of fixed capital remains constant. We have determined the shares of wages and profits as well as the rate of profit on capital quite independently of the principles of marginal productivity.

P. Samuelson (1967: 715) emphasised the central proposition of neo-classical theory of value: "Capital–labour up: interest or profit rate down: wage rate up: capital–output up." Kaldor (1975: 356) has argued: "These propositions are *only* true in a world of homogeneous and linear production functions, where an increase in capital relative to labour increases output less than proportionately. In reality this is not so: higher wage rates in terms of products are associated with higher capital–labour ratios but are *not* associated with higher capital–output ratios."

Kalecki and Keynes held to the idea that equilibrium in a capitalist economy with unemployment is quite possible and, without state intervention, even unavoidable. Our model typically yields the persistence of unemployment as well. The model explains why wages continue to rise even when there is significant unemployment. Unlike Kaldor (1957), we do not postulate full employment. The rate of profit on capital depends on the coefficients of the technical progress function that, in turn, determine the rate of growth of labour productivity.

The higher the equilibrium rate of productivity growth $m_1/(1 - m_2)$, the higher the equilibrium share of wages in the national income (u_2), the employment ratio (v_2, if $b < 1$) and the rate of profit (M_2/K_2) and the lower the capital–output ratio (s_2). Thus, for the model economy, a failure to innovate is detrimental to employment, real wages and profitability, whereas increasing technical dynamism is favourable for them.

It is interesting to compare some of our conclusions with those drawn in modern neo-classical concepts of cyclical growth. These concepts postulate, first, that the rational behaviour of entrepreneurs is aimed at adjusting the capital–output ratio to its optimal level; second, the fixed-point equilibrium in neo-classical models does not depend on the speed of this adjustment. The neo-classical approach does not apply the idea of capitalists' bounded rationality, therefore it abstracts from social learning.

Van der Ploeg (1985: 225) has relaxed Goodwin's assumption about a constant capital–output ratio by having firms maximise profits subject to a constant elasticity of substitution (CES) production function and come to the interesting conclusion: "For the general CES technology, the equilibrium share of wages in the national income is a decreasing function of the natural rate of growth . . . .." The same result has been obtained in a model with a neo-classical flavour, where a technical progress function and profit-maximising hypothesis have been used.

Our formula (3.24) provides us with a different conclusion: the equilibrium share of wages in the national income (u_2) is an increasing function of the natural rate of growth which equals the rate of productivity growth $m_1/(1 - m_2)$ for a constant labour force ($n = 0$). This seemingly paradoxical and at first counter-intuitive result explains Goodwin's observation quoted as the epigraph to this chapter.[1]

At fixed-point equilibrium in the extended neo-classical model, the warranted and natural rates of growth equal the sum of labour supply growth and productivity growth, while real wages and productivity grow at the same rate; the higher the equilibrium rate of productivity growth, the greater the employment ratio and profitability, just as in our model.

Our results are similar to the neo-classical conditions necessary for convergence to steady-state growth: a constant profit rate and constant income distribution between labour and capital. In the modern neo-classical model in contrast to the post-Marxian model, the higher the equilibrium rate of productivity growth due to non-autonomous technical progress, the lower the equilibrium share of wages in the national income ($1 - m_2$) and — for a definite range of the parameters — the higher the capital–output ratio.

Neither approach suggests curbing productivity growth to preserve jobs. An increase in employment can occur without a decline in the rate of real wages. Still, the implications for economic policy from the two models are substantially different.

The neo-classical model explicitly displays the "high" equilibrium labour bill share as the culprit for the "low" pace of technological progress in the long run. Thus, neo-classical economics would prescribe a diminishing of this share in order to achieve a higher economic growth rate over a business cycle or long wave. This course of action is mostly confrontation-oriented. It is not generally valid. Income inequality does grow during the depression and recovery phases of the long wave, but social policies that increase inequities even further could have very damaging effects for the social fabric.

The average profit rate, employment ratio and labour bill share in net output could be raised in the post-Marxian model over a business cycle or long wave by shifting the technical progress function upwards. Post-Marxian economic theory directs policy-makers to "win–win" solutions via an innovation offensive and better governance. The recommended policy has to be mainly consensus-, not confrontation-oriented (cf. Sterman 1992).

Environmental aspects of economic growth go beyond the scope of this chapter. It is worthy of note that the continuous exponential advance in technology at 4% per year eliminates all the assumed limits in the model World3 (see Meadows *et al.* 1974: 524). An additional requirement in this global model for such unbounded expansion is that technology advances at no cost.

If our model economy starts at the steady state, it grows exponentially, $P_t = P_0 \exp((1 - u_2)/s_2)$. A declining rate of growth of the effective labour supply due to a shorter working day, and a slower increase in the population can retard economic growth.

Different bottlenecks (like shortages of particular skills and natural resources), the impossibility of substituting certain natural resources by products of labour may slow growth even further. If institutional, thermodynamic and ecological factors (such as the depletion of the ozone layer, global warming, downfall of biodiversity and others) become incompatible with exponential growth, it will be necessary to change the very pattern of evolution to guarantee the sustainable development of humanity (see Chapter 6).

4.2   THE CAUSAL-LOOP STRUCTURE OF THE MODEL

A lot of the credit must go to Marx for his efforts to use the available, mostly linear, mathematics for supporting a sustained theoretical penetration of the economic organism. Being in a more favourable position, I can use elements of the theory of nonlinear differential equations to express my views on capital accumulation.

Let us place our model in a nonlinear co-operative–competitive network. Let G be an open subset of R^n. A differential equation $\dot{x} = f(x)$ defined on $G \subseteq R^n$ is *co-operative* if $\partial f_i(x)/\partial x_j \geq 0$ for all $x \in G$ and all $i \neq j$ (the growth of every component is enhanced by an increase in any other component). *Competitive* systems are defined by $\partial f_i(x)/\partial x_j \leq 0$ for all $i \neq j$ (see Hofbauer and Sigmund 1988: 158). The system (3.21)–(3.23) represents a mixed case, i.e. a *competitive–co-operative* system in a three-dimensional phase space:

$$\partial f_1(s)/\partial v = 0, \qquad \partial f_1(s)/\partial u = (1 - m_2)n_2 s \begin{cases} \leq 0, & \text{if } m_2 \geq 1, \quad n_2 \geq 0 \\ > 0, & \text{if } m_2 < 1, \quad n_2 > 0 \end{cases}$$

$$\partial f_2(v)/\partial s = -(1 - u)v/s^2 < 0, \qquad \partial f_2(v)/\partial u = -v/s - n_2 v < 0$$

$$\partial f_3(u)/\partial s = 0, \qquad \partial f_3(u)/\partial v = ru > 0.$$

To my knowledge, no global theorems have yet been proved about these mixed competitive–co-operative feedback networks (see Grossberg 1988: 38). In the three-and-higher-dimensional case the Poincaré–Bendixson theorem cannot be applied.

Note that the labour bill share (the main "predator") adversely affects growth of the employment ratio (the prey) and, if $m_2 < 1$ and $n_2 > 0$, it activates growth of the capital–output ratio. This ratio (the second "predator") inhibits the growth of the employment ratio. The rising employment ratio is promoting the growth of the labour bill share. The system has fairly satisfactory self-regulating properties under certain restrictions on its parameters.

It is known that the majority of dynamic systems in economics belong to the class of dissipative systems. The characteristic property of a dissipative system implies that the volume of an element of the phase space shrinks to zero as time progresses, when trajectories approach an attractor. Formally, this property can be examined with the help of the Lie derivative or the divergence defined as

$$\dot{V}/V = \text{div}(f) = \sum \partial f_i / \partial x_i, \quad i = 1, \ldots, 3, \tag{4.11}$$

with V as the "volume" and div (f) as the divergence of f. The Lie derivative is negative when the system is dissipative. One of the important properties of a dissipative system is time irreversibility on transients to attractors (see Lorenz 1989: 55–56, 63).

In our model the Lie derivative is calculated as follows:

$$\dot{V}/V = \hat{s} + \hat{v} + \hat{u} + (b - m_2)n_2u \tag{4.12}$$

$$= (-m_1 - (m_2 - 1)(n_1 + n_2u)) + ((1 - u)/s - (n_1 + n_2u) - n)$$

$$+ (-g + rv - m_1 + n_1(b - m_2) + 2(b - m_2)n_2u)$$

$$= -2m_1 + (n_1 + n_2u)(-2m_2 + b) + (b - m_2)n_2u$$

$$+ (1 - u)/s - n - g + rv. \tag{4.13}$$

Let us now consider the local behaviour of the solution of the unforced continuous-time nonlinear system

$$\dot{x} = f(x) \tag{4.14}$$

near the equilibrium $E_2(x_2 = (s_2, v_2, u_2))$ in R^3. The linear equation

$$\dot{y} = Jy, \tag{4.15}$$

where J is the Jacobian, can be solved explicitly.

At the fixed-point equilibrium $(\dot{s}, \dot{v}, \dot{u}) = 0$ and $\dot{V}/V = (b - m_2)n_2u < 0$ (for $b < m_2$ and $n_2 > 0$). Damping closely associates with the decreasing amplitude of oscillations, in particular due to the term $(b - m_2)n_2u$ in (4.12).

The following constellation of coefficients has been chosen as illustration:

$$m_1 = 0.12, \qquad m_2 = 0.8, \qquad n_1 = 0.12, \qquad n_2 = 1.5,$$

$$r = 1.8, \qquad b = 0.2, \qquad g = 1, \qquad n = 0.02.$$

The requirement of local stability (3.37) has not been infringed. This allows us to apply the theorem of Hartman and Grobman (see Steeb and Kunick 1989: 39–40) which states that both systems (4.14) and (4.15) are topologically equivalent in a sufficiently small neighbourhood of the fixed point (E_2).

The chosen constellation of coefficients gives rise to the following equilibrium values of our state variables:

$$s_2 \cong 1.0968, \qquad v_2 \cong 0.822, \qquad u_2 = 0.32.$$

We have found that E_2 is hyperbolic in the sense that all eigenvalues of J have non-vanishing real parts. Because the real parts of the eigenvalues are all negative, the equilibrium E_2 is a sink. Moreover, it is locally *asymptotically stable*.

After the initial point has been displaced from the fixed point, the converging fluctuations arise (for example, $s_0 = s_2$, $v_0 = 0.722$, $u_0 = u_2$). The period of fluctuations is about six years (see Figure 4.1). The labour bill share peaks at a value of 0.36 at year 4.4 and 0.34 at year 10.4. The damping ratio, defined relative to the mean point of the oscillation, is therefore approximately (see Mass 1975: 52)

$$1 - (0.34 - 0.32)/(0.36 - 0.32) = 0.5.$$

The model yields the negative Lie derivative (see Figure 4.2) for this case, illustrating the smaller distance between the orbits.

Any upward or downward deviations in the vicinity of the fixed point will lead to smaller deviations, since any divergence will set up forces tending to eliminate it. The system tends in this region of the parameters' values towards the equilibrium rate of economic growth at which the natural and warranted rates of growth are equal. The divergence of the two in the vicinity of an unstable equilibrium is characteristic of Harrod's growth model (the so-called knife-edge property). Notice that a natural rate of growth, exogenously given in Harrod's growth model, is determined partially endogenously in our model.

Figures 4.3–4.6 depict the stock-and-flow feedback structure of the model. Solid arrows identify real additions, broken arrows are used for information links.

The boxes containing the main variables are joined by arrows. An arrow going from one box to another means that the variable in the latter box is a function of that in the former. A sign of a partial derivative is also given.

It becomes clear from inspecting the diagrams that the model has two main and three small feedback loops. The initial main loop connects the relative wage and the employment

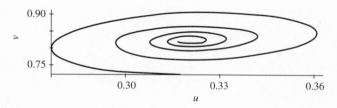

Figure 4.1 The fluctuations converging to the steady state in the dissipative system

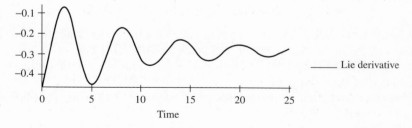

Figure 4.2 The Lie derivative for the dissipative system

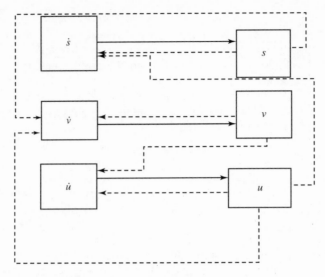

Figure 4.3   The causal-loop structure of the model

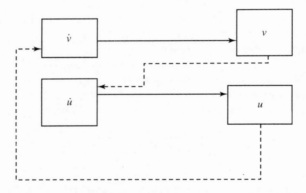

Figure 4.4   The first main loop of the model. (Note: The polarity of this loop is negative.)

ratio, the additional main loop is of a higher order of complexity — the relative wage, employment ratio and capital–output ratio. The small loops involve s, v and u individually. Integration of $\dot{s}$, $\dot{v}$, $\dot{u}$ creates the implicit delays mentioned earlier. As the partial derivatives $\partial f_i/\partial x_i$, $i = 1, \ldots, 3$, change their signs, the polarity of each feedback loop alters.

The main feedback loops are balancing. The forms of proportional and derivative feedback control, used in the model economy, are not sufficient to eliminate deviations from the fixed-point equilibrium entirely and tend to cause fluctuations.

A network of excitatory and inhibitory neurones connected by synapses in the brain and central nervous system has similar peculiarities (see Thompson 1987: 54–55). So it is not just pure coincidence that brain rhythms and economic fluctuations are modelled by the same mathematical structure known as a limit cycle (see below). A limit cycle is a more advanced notion of equilibrium than a steady state.

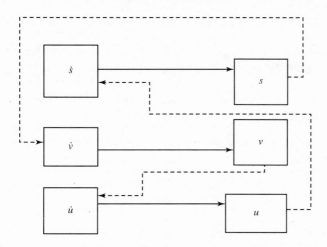

Figure 4.5   The second main loop of the model. (Note: The polarity of this loop is negative for $m_2 < 1$ and $n_2 > 0$.)

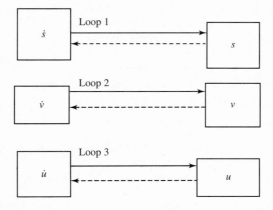

Figure 4.6   The alternating polarity of the small loops within the model. (Note: The dominant polarity of loop 1 is determined by sign $[u - u_2]$, loop 2 by sign $[(1 - u)/s - (n_1 + n_2 u) - n]$, loop 3 by sign$[-g + rv - m_1 + n_1(b - m_2) + 2(b - m_2)n_2 u]$.)

The Hopf theorem may constitute the only tool to establish the existence of closed orbits. In this study of the cyclical motion we choose b (see equation (3.13)) as a bifurcation (control) parameter, although it is possible to select either. The inequality (3.37) turns into equality if

$$b_0 = m_2 - (n_1 + n_2 - \tilde{w})(1 - m_2)(\tilde{w} + n)/[(\tilde{w} - n_1)(n_1 + n_2 + n)]. \qquad (4.16)$$

The Hopf theorem establishes only the existence of closed orbits in a neighbourhood of x^* at $b = b_0$, and it does not clarify the stability of orbits, which may arise on either side of b_0.

Consider the equilibrium of the system (4.14) as dependent on b:

$$\dot{x} = 0 = f(x, b). \qquad (4.17)$$

The determinant of the Jacobian matrix (J) differs from zero in our case for any possible equilibrium (x, b) if $v_2 r u_2 n_2 s_2 (m_2 - 1) \neq 0$. This requirement is typically satisfied.

The implicit function theorem ensures that for every b in a neighbourhood $B_r(b_0) \in R$ of the parameter value b_0 there exists a unique equilibrium x^*. Changes of b do not affect s_2 and u_2, whereas v_2 diminishes if b grows.

We assume that this equilibrium is stable for small values of the parameter b and the other properties are satisfied:

(i)   the Jacobian of (4.14) has a pair of pure imaginary eigenvalues and no other eigen-
      values with zero real parts,
(ii) the derivative

$$\frac{d(\text{Re } \lambda(b))}{db} > 0 \quad \text{for } b = b_0.$$

Then there exists some periodic solution bifurcating from $x^*(b_0)$ at $b = b_0$ and the period of fluctuations is near $2\pi/\beta_0$ ($\beta_0 = \lambda(b_0)/i$). If a closed orbit is an attractor, it is usually called a *limit cycle* (cf. Lorenz 1989: 76–77).

Please note that the credit for the discovery of limit cycles goes to A. Poincaré (1854–1912). A. A. Andronov and S. E. Khaikin investigated a bifurcation of a steady state into a limit cycle in the 1930s earlier than E. Hopf, so the notion "Hopf's bifurcation" could be misleading. It is used in this book only for brevity.

A pattern of economic evolution generated via the Hopf bifurcation differs in many respects from the pattern of converging fluctuations. The following sections pay attention to this difference. The relationships between the natural, warranted and actual rates are studied in section 5.3, in particular.

4.3   PITFALLS OF BARGAINING DELAYS

> Obstructing the doors causes delay and may be dangerous.
>
> (The warning in the London Tube)

According to John Sculley, the modern reorganisation of work could prove as massive and wrenching as the Industrial Revolution. We agree with the experts who warn that these changes can only arise with social frictions (see Ehrbar and Roth 1993).

The system dynamics approach is useful for a better understanding of contests among social classes and industrial disputes between management and labour. It can be a helpful instrument in negotiating. A system dynamics model of a contest or dispute may be a part of an education process as well. We will address this problem in the context of social bargaining by applying a case study approach. Being mostly interested in the macroeconomic consequences of a period of bargaining we will treat the bargaining as a "black box" at a rather high level of abstraction (see Ryzhenkov 1994a, b).

For illustration, suppose the behaviour of the modelling system is influenced by labour contract terms. Let us consider an elicited response to an introduction of a wage delay in the modified Phillips equation (3.13). It may be "caused by the extension of collective bargaining and particularly by the growth of arbitration and conciliation procedures" (Phillips 1958: 293). Note that the anticipation of social tensions may lead to an abnormal

Table 4.1   The hypothetical learning dichotomy in the
model economy[a]

Learning		
involuntary		voluntary
Response		
elicited		emitted
Change of behaviour		
reactive		operative

[a]Based on Berger (1970).

increase in real wages, but we will not take this aspect into account. Table 4.1 depicts the hypothetical learning dichotomy in the model economy.

C. Chiarella (1990) has introduced a time delay into the wage formation equation of the original Goodwin model. The real Phillips curve is: (a) without a delay

$$\hat{w} = -\gamma + \rho v \quad (\gamma > 0, \rho > 0)$$

(b) with an exponentially distributed information delay T (years)

$$\hat{w} = -\gamma + \rho x,$$

where

$$\dot{x} = (v - x)/T, \qquad x(t) = \int_{-\infty}^{t} \frac{e^{-(t-\tau)/T}}{T} v(\tau) \, d(\tau).$$

Now assume that $\hat{w}$ is a positive function of $x(t)$, a continuously distributed weighted average of the employment rate over past periods. The weighting function is a declining exponential. The parameter T is the mean time delay. In the limit $T \to 0$, $x(t) = v(t)$. The inverse $1/T$ (year)$^{-1}$ is the speed of adjustment.

J. Forrester (1969: 349) writes: "The effects of a delay depend on where it is in the system. Delays may produce either amplification or attenuation of disturbances depending on where they appear." We have already used the simple exponential delay many times in equations of the general form

$$\dot{Y} = \delta[Z(t) - Y(t)],$$

where δ represents the speed of adjustment of the variable $Y(t)$ to its desired, or equilibrium, value $Z(t)$.[2]

The Goodwin model is the two-dimensional system

$$\dot{v} = ((1/s - (\alpha + \beta)) - u/s)v,$$

$$\dot{u} = (-(\alpha + \gamma) + \rho v)u,$$

where s is the capital–output ratio, u the share of labour in national income, v the rate of employment, α the rate of technical progress and β the rate of growth of the labour force (see Goodwin 1972).

The equilibrium in Goodwin's model is stable (it is not yet asymptotically stable). Except for the equilibrium and the coordinate axes, every trajectory obtained with this model is a closed orbit that crosses the initial point. Each such phase trajectory has its own periodic time. The initial point in the phase space may be chosen more or less arbitrarily. These closed orbits are neither asymptotically nor structurally stable (this means that small variations in the magnitudes of the coefficients are capable of destroying the cyclical pattern). Thus there are some reasons for further development of this model. A more realistic set of equations could be expected to yield structurally stable focuses and limit cycles. Note that the mathematical study of structural stability was initiated in Russia by A. A. Andronov and L. S. Pontrjagin in the 1930s.

The extended Goodwin model with the explicit time delay in wage formation becomes (see Chiarella 1990: 71–73)

$$\dot{x} = (v - x)/T$$
$$\dot{v} = ((1/s - (\alpha + \beta)) - u/s)v,$$
$$\dot{u} = (-(\alpha + \gamma) + \rho x)u,$$

where $\gamma > 0$, $\rho > 0$, $T > 0$.

It has been shown by use of the centre-manifold theory that the resulting system of three differential equations displays stable limit cycle behaviour at least for a relatively small time delay (see Chiarella 1990: 70–80). However, the dynamic properties in the model for larger values of the time delay have not yet been investigated.

To continue the work of Chiarella we now turn to case studies. Four of the case studies consider elementary bargaining over automating/wage/employment/timing of innovation (separately), and the fifth analyses simultaneous bargaining over all of these issues. In numerical simulations we have used first-order and third-order exponential delays, represented by the DYNAMO built-in functions SMOOTH and DLINF3, respectively.

The third-order delay is equivalent to three cascaded single-order delays, with each single-order delay having a delay time of DEL/3, where DEL is the same total average delay (see Forrester 1969: 86–92). The transient responses to changes in flow rate usually differ.

In particular, wage change will be related not to the current employment ratio, but to the ratio lagged, on average, by several months. An explosive cyclical motion around the trend may be obtained, for example, by DEL = 0.25 (three months) in both cases (see Figure 4.7).

Note that this example and that of the six-year cycle above have the same constellation of other coefficients and initial values. The amplitude of oscillations grows faster if the model is extended by the third-order delay. As a result of introducing the delay, the system becomes considerably less stable. This sensitivity shows that the wage delay is one of

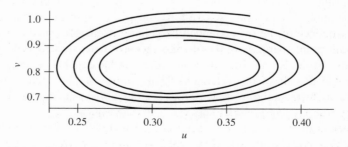

Figure 4.7   Diverging fluctuations in the system with the information delay

Table 4.2   Effects of the bargaining delays

Elementary bargaining	Variable	Factor	Delay (years)	Fluctuations
Wage	$\hat{w}$	v	0.25	Exploding
			0.18	Converging
Automating	$\hat{K/L}$	u	0.25	Converging
Innovating	$\hat{a}$	$\hat{K/L}$	0.25	Converging
Employment	$\hat{v}$	$\hat{a}$	0.25	Converging
Simultaneous			0.25	Exploding
bargaining			0.10	Converging

Notes:
1. The equilibrium: $(s_2, u_2, v_2) = (1.0968, 0.32, 0.822)$.
2. The initial vector $(s_2, u_2, v_2 - 0.1)$.
3. The magnitudes of the parameters: $m_1 = 0.12$, $m_2 = 0.8$, $n_1 = 0.12$, $n_2 = 1.5$, $r = 1.8$, $b = 0.2$, $g = 1$, $n = 0.02$.
4. It is not implied that this purely illustrative constellation is in fact empirically accurate.

the most crucial parameters in determining the system's dynamic performance. Table 4.2 summarises the results of our case studies.

We observe that delays which do not harm stability in elementary bargaining, under an illustrative constellation of the parameters and the initial conditions of the model, may violate stability in simultaneous bargaining. In order to guarantee stability and technological advance, the latter should be less lengthy than the former.

Our findings maintain the Phillips results that a comparatively small change in the time forms of the delays may have a great effect on the stability of a closed-loop control system, especially if the values of the correction factors are high (see Phillips 1957: 270–271). In particular, the longer the time delays in the responses around the main control loop, the less effective is derivative control.

Under the conditions explicitly formulated, the dynamics of the model are locally stable in the neighbourhood of its equilibrium. These dynamics are not robust with respect to definite changes in social relations.

Note that an introduction of information delays not only raises a dimensionality of the system of differential equations but alters the Routh–Hourwitz conditions of local stability as well. The non-trivial equilibrium of the system is, of course, also an equilibrium of the similar system with a higher dimensionality, but at the present stage of investigation we are not considering its stability properties.[3]

It is known that the outcome of bargaining is either an agreement about the terms of mutual co-operation or a conflict. As we have seen, a conflict may be an unintended or intended consequence of the overextended bargaining itself. This practically and conceptually important point (bargaining length) has recently been studied in the experimental gaming context by B. Kuon. She has come to a similar conclusion (Kuon 1994: 144): "It is remarkable that the average length of bargaining for plays that ended in conflict is about twice as long as the average length for plays that ended in agreement. This is approximately true for every game type."

The parameters of the model have been chosen to facilitate the computer simulation without matching real-world conditions. Still, the model, perhaps grotesquely, mirrors the social contradictions. A society only capable of involuntary learning is condemned to experience escalating conflicts, as has been illustrated. One should keep in mind, however, that growing systems usually develop in the direction of more elaborated adjustment processes (see Miller 1978: 108–109).

A conflict itself may be regarded as a learning process. "Case studies and comparative anecdotal evidence suggest that unions and works councils do not generally impede technological change, reduce labour-management conflict, lower quit rates, and facilitate improved communication between management and workers," L. Kenworthy (1995: 147) writes.

In a democratic society, industrial conflicts usually end when the potential settlement opportunities are conceived as more attractive than continued open discord. The real uncertainty and deterministic chaos (still hypothetical) in economic data complicate learning and a policy design. The higher organisational complexity requires a better governance in order to minimise a risk of mismanagement, whereby collective bargaining plays a certain role.

The delays introduced in this section are not necessarily connected exclusively with bargaining. I noted earlier that they may be brought about by other factors as well, including fixed cost outlays for labour power, rules of labour contracts imposed by the state, etc.

4.4   FREE OSCILLATIONS RESULTING FROM STRUCTURAL CHANGES

The inequality (3.37) turns into equality if

$$m_2 - b_0 = (1 - u_2)(1 - m_2)/(u_2(n_2 s_2 + 1)), \tag{4.18}$$

where $1 > u_2 > 0$, $n_2 > 0$ and $b_0 < m_2 < 1$. For this critical magnitude (b_0) the equilibrium employment ratio is given by

$$v_2 = (g + m_1 + (m_2 - b_0)(n_2 + n_2 u_2))/r$$

$$= (g + m_1 + (m_2 - b_0)\tilde{w})/r$$

$$= \frac{g + m_1}{r} + \frac{\tilde{w}}{r} \frac{(1 - u_2)(1 - m_2)}{u_2(n_2 s_2 + 1)}$$

$$= \frac{g + m_1}{r} + \frac{\tilde{w}}{r} \left(\frac{(1 - u_2)(1 - m_2)}{u_2 \left(\dfrac{n_1 + n_2 - \tilde{w}}{\tilde{w} + n} + 1 \right)} \right)$$

$$= \frac{g + m_1}{r} + \frac{m_1}{r} \frac{\dfrac{1 - u_2}{u_2}}{\left(\dfrac{n_1 + n_2 - \tilde{w}}{\tilde{w} + n} + 1 \right)}$$

$$= \frac{g + m_1}{r} + \frac{m_1}{r} \left(\frac{\dfrac{n_1 + n_2 - \tilde{w}}{\tilde{w} - n_1}}{\dfrac{n_1 + n_2 - \tilde{w}}{\tilde{w} + n} + 1} \right)$$

$$= \frac{g + m_1 + m_1 \dfrac{(\tilde{w} + n)(n_1 + n_2 - \tilde{w})}{(\tilde{w} - n_1)(n_1 + n_2 + n)}}{r}. \tag{4.19}$$

The characteristic polynomial for $b = b_0$ is

$$\lambda^3 + a_2\lambda^2 + a_1\lambda + a_1a_2 = \lambda^2(\lambda + a_2) + a_1(\lambda + a_2)$$

$$= (\lambda + a_2)(\lambda^2 + a_1) = 0. \tag{4.20}$$

It has the following roots:

$$\lambda_1 = -a_2 = -(m_2 - b)n_2u_2 < 0, \quad \text{if } n_2 > 0 \text{ and } m_2 > b; \tag{4.21}$$

$$\lambda_{2,3} = \pm i\sqrt{-a_1} = \pm i\sqrt{ru_2v_2(1/s_2 + n_2)}$$

$$= \pm i\sqrt{\frac{ru_2\left(g + m_1 + m_1\dfrac{(\tilde{w} + n)(n_1 + n_2 - \tilde{w})}{(\tilde{w} - n_1)(n_1 + n_2 + n)}\right)\dfrac{n_2(n_1 + n_2 + n)}{n_1 + n_2 - \tilde{w}}}{r}}$$

$$= \pm i\sqrt{\left[(\tilde{w} - n_1)\frac{(n_1 + n_2 + n)(g + m_1)}{(n_1 + n_2 - \tilde{w})} + m_1(\tilde{w} + n)\right]}. \tag{4.22}$$

(Equations (3.24) and (4.19) have been used.)

The period of oscillation near $x^*(b_0)$ is about $2\pi/\sqrt{-a_1}$ (years). In the original Goodwin model it is about $2\pi/(s^{-1}\rho v_eu_e)^{1/2}$ years, where $s = \text{const}$, $u_e = 1 - s(\alpha + \beta)$, $v_e = (\alpha + \gamma)/\rho$. Solow (1990: 40) says: "Since the model determines its own period, there is room for some interplay between the facts and the theoretical structure."

One should not overlook that the approximate period of fluctuations near E_2 is independent of b in our model. Assuming $g + m_1 > 0$, the higher the rate of technological progress and rate of growth of the labour force, the shorter this period; it is longer, the higher the rate of growth of capital intensity (as a function of the two structural coefficients n_1 and n_2). The trade-off between stability and the period may therefore be the subject of economic policy-making. In particular, if technological advance and productivity growth remain laggard, stabilising the world economy by accelerated capital deepening may lengthen the depression phase of the current Kondratiev cycle globally.

Let us take coefficients and initial values, besides b, from our example in section 4.2 ($m_1 = 0.12$, $m_2 = 0.8$, $n_1 = 0.12$, $n_2 = 1.5$, $r = 1.8$, $g = 1$, $n = 0.02$; $s_0 = 1.0968$, $v_0 = 0.722$, $u_0 = 0.32$) and $b_0 \approx 0.63933$. The Jacobian of (4.15) has one pair of pure imaginary eigenvalues ($\alpha \pm \beta i$) and no other eigenvalues with zero real parts (moreover, at the point $b = b_0$ $d\alpha/db > 0$). According to the Hopf bifurcation theorem (the existence part), there exist some periodic solutions bifurcating from $x^*(b_0)$ at b_0 (see Table 4.3).

The stability properties of the closed orbits depend on nonlinear terms. This issue will not be treated analytically in depth in this book. Computer simulations will again be helpful.

Further increasing b (at $b = 0.73$) provides us with one real negative eigenvalue and a conjugate pair of eigenvalues with positive real components. It means that the corresponding fixed point is the saddle (see Table 4.3).

If $b = m_2 = 0.8$, i.e. when b is higher than the threshold (b_0), the sign of the Lie derivative periodically changes. At $b = 0.82$ there is the saddle-focus (cf. Wiggins 1990: 553).

Our computer simulations have shown that the initial system of the ordinary differential equations seems to be more stable than its linear approximation in the neighbourhood of the equilibrium under the above constellation of coefficients and the chosen initial

Table 4.3 The influence of the value of the control parameter (b) on the equilibrium properties

Bifurcation parameter b	Eigenvalues		Derivative $d\alpha/db$	Equilibrium (x^*, b)
	Real λ	Conjugate pair $(\alpha \pm \beta i)$		
0.2	−0.078	−0.105 ± 1.06i	0.28	Locally and asymptotically stable
0.3	−0.078	−0.081 ± 1.04i	0.27	Locally and asymptotically stable
0.63933	−0.077	0 ± 0.97i	0.26	Non-hyperbolic, non-stable[a]
0.73	−0.077	0.022 ± 0.95i	0.25	The saddle (the saddle of index 2)
0.8	−0.077	0.038 ± 0.93i	0.24	The saddle (the saddle of index 2)[b]

[a] There is the Hopf bifurcation: the existence of closed orbits in a neighbourhood of (x^*, b_0).
[b] See Thompson (1987: 35).

magnitudes of the main parameters u, v and s (the nonlinear system exhibits converging fluctuations even if b is greater than b_0 but smaller than 0.73).

Another possible scenario for a Hopf bifurcation might be by changing n_2. It follows from (3.37) that the critical value of this coefficient is given by the formula

$$
n_2^c = -\frac{\dfrac{(1 - m_2)}{(m_2 - b)} + \dfrac{\dfrac{n_1 + n}{m_1}}{1 - m_2} + n}{\dfrac{1}{\dfrac{m_1}{1 - m_2} + n} - \dfrac{1 - m_2}{(m_2 - b)\left(\dfrac{m_1}{1 - m_2} - n_1\right)}}, \tag{4.23}
$$

If $n_1 = 0$ and $b = 0$, we have a simpler expression:

$$
n_2^c = -\frac{\dfrac{1 - m_2}{m_2} + \dfrac{\dfrac{n}{m_1}}{1 - m_2} + n}{\dfrac{1}{\dfrac{m_1}{1 - m_2} + n} - \dfrac{1 - m_2}{m_2 \dfrac{m_1}{1 - m_2}}}. \tag{4.24}
$$

The last expression is not defined for $n = 0$, if $m_2 = 0.5$ and/or $m_1 = 0$.

For $m_1 = 0.02$, $m_2 = 0.5$, $n_1 = 0.01$, $r = 0.062$, $b = 0.1$, $g = 0.02$, $n = 0.02$, the choice of $n_2 \approx 0.07$ produces a bifurcation into a closed orbit. Numerical experiments display a transient to a specific regular and sustained limit cycle depending on the initial conditions.

Liapunov characteristic exponents measure the average rate at which orbits, which are close initially, separate (Wiggins 1990: 603–615). Using the Wolf algorithm we have calculated the Liapunov characteristic exponents for different magnitudes of the model parameters (see Wolf 1986). We have not found that the values of the parameters satisfy the normal requirements that would generate deterministic chaos.

Van der Ploeg (1983: 243, 247) has shown that the speed of substitution activities (ξ) may be used as a bifurcation parameter in his model of the conflict over distribution of income. The system exhibits damped cycles for small enough ξ and monotonic convergence for fast or even immediate adjustment of the capital–output ratio ($\xi = \infty$). So the cyclical form of motion is not an immanent characteristic of growth in the neo-classical model.

Zhang (1988) has utilised the Hopf theorem to prove that limit cycles appear near a fixed-point equilibrium as this parameter passes the critical value in that model. He has presented general conditions for the existence of limit cycles and found period and stability conditions. In particular, there are sufficient conditions for the Hopf bifurcation to occur near the equilibrium for the critical magnitude $\xi_0 = \gamma + \tilde{w} + n$, where $\gamma \geq 0$.

For $m_2 = 0.5$, $u_2 = m_1/(n_2(1 - m_2)) - n_1/n_2 = 1 - m_2$, and $\xi = (m_1 - 0.5n_1)$, the Ploeg–Zhang model and my model contain the same differential equation for $\dot{s}$. The differential equations for $\dot{v}$ and $\dot{u}$ can be made identical in both models by choosing appropriate values of the parameters (in particular, $\gamma = 0$, $b = 0$).

The Zhang results are not directly applicable to our model even in this particular case (for $n \geq 0$). When the two models formally coincide, our analogue of ξ is less than $\tilde{w}$: $m_1 - n_1(1 - m_2) < \tilde{w}$ if $n_1 > 0$. (For $0 < m_2 < 1$ and $n_1 = 0$, the two requirements $u_2 = m_1/(n_2(1 - m_2)) = 0.5$ and $m_1 = \tilde{w}$ are not compatible.) This contradicts the Zhang sufficient requirement for the Hopf bifurcation to occur. Moreover, the neo-classical model postulates $(1 - m_2)$ to be the equilibrium relative wage independently of ξ. In our model changes in the compound coefficient $(m_1 - n_1(1 - m_2))$ typically affect the equilibrium relative wage (u_2). That is why we have looked for another solution for generating auto-oscillations in our model.

Zhang (1988) has held the view that the capital–output ratio decreases from its maximal magnitude, while the share of labour in net income increases from its average value during a business cycle. After arriving at the maximal value the labour share begins to decrease, while the capital–output ratio keeps decreasing.

It can be easily shown via computer simulations that this interpretation is hardly true: the moving of these variables on the plane has the opposite direction in his model. Still my critique of the neo-classical approach goes further than demonstrating this error. Its main shortcoming is the assumption of no dependency between the speed of substitution of capital for labour and the steady-state dynamic equilibrium. I have demonstrated that this speed is determined endogenously in the post-Marxian model.

The neo-classical growth theory represents a ratio of profit rate to a unit real wage as a function of capital intensity. For brevity, let us take a case without technical progress. Its graphic on a plane is represented by a curve that is sloping down (Jones 1976: 34–35, 174–176). In my model, this connection is only typical for the recession phase of the long wave.

To be specific, we assume the following magnitudes for the Andronov–Hopf bifurcation: $m_1 = 0$, $m_2 = 0$, $n_1 = -0.01$, $n_2 = 0.0106$, $r = 0.02$, $b_0 \approx -0.058\,2524$, $g = 0.018$, $n = 0.02$; the equilibrium vector $(s_2, u_2, v_2) \approx (3, 0.94, 0.9)$, the initial vector $(s_0, u_0, v_0) = (3, 0.94, 0.91)$. The period is about 80 years (longer than Kondratiev's).

Careful examination of computer simulations shows that the outlined neo-classical connection is observed only during the recession phase of the long wave (see Figures 4.8 and 4.9). So our model generalises the early neo-classical presentation.

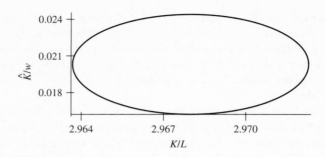

Figure 4.8   The responsiveness of the profit rate–unit real wage ratio $(\hat{K}/w)$ to changes of capital intensity (K/L). Counter-clockwise

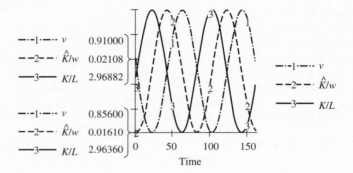

Figure 4.9   The phasing of the profit rate–unit real wage ratio $(\hat{K}/w)$, the employment ratio (v) and capital intensity (K/L). The normalised view

The main model variables (the relative wage, employment and capital–output ratios) have no trend. The determination of a secular trend in economic activity, i.e. a general tendency in a specific direction, is a by-product of obtaining the equations of motion for these variables. It is shown that even more lengthy long-term economic fluctuations than Kondratiev's cycles could exist in the earlier phases of emerging capitalism (before the Industrial Revolution unfolded at the end of the eighteenth century in England). This approach to the model economy is free from perspectivistic distortion in empirical studies resulting from a mechanistic (non-dialectic) separation of the trend and the long waves in statistical data (see Reijnders 1990).

   R.M. Goodwin (1990: 70–71, 102–130) has used a system in the form proposed by Rössler

$$\dot{v} = -du + fu - ez$$

$$\dot{u} = +hv$$

$$\dot{z} = b + gz(v - c),$$

where v and u are the deviations of the employment ratio and relative wage from the equilibrium values and a third variable z is a control parameter. Note that the

Goodwin equations for u and v, unlike our equations (3.22)–(3.23), do not have non-linear terms. Business cycles and long waves can be generated simultaneously in his system. By a careful choice of parameters and initial conditions, the Rössler–Goodwin system exhibits irregular fluctuations. However, that chaotic growth-oscillator is neither complicated enough, nor realistic enough, according to Goodwin's own judgement (see Goodwin 1990: 70–71, 102–130).

Goodwin also generated business cycles and long waves simultaneously by another method. He used a chaotic attractor, adding an exogenous 50-year logistic of innovation in a Rössler-like system of three differential equations with only one nonlinearity. Such an exogenous procedure is not quite satisfactory for a theory of endogenous long waves.

Perhaps our difficulties in finding initial conditions and parameters that would render irregular fluctuations in the extended model (3.21)–(3.23) are explained by the higher efficacy of its more advanced self-regulation. Its ability to withstand external shocks without losing self organisation has not been studied, however.

It is not yet quite clear whether or not real macroeconomic data on employment, income distribution and the capital–output ratio exhibit deterministic chaos. Exogenous shocks complicate the subject matter even more. This aspect requires further investigation.

In conclusion to this section, it is reasonable to remember the Kalecki (1939) idea: "Future inquiry into problems of growth should be directed ... towards treating also the coefficients used in our equations as slowly changing variables rooted in the past development of the system."

NOTES

1. It was not analytically derived by him but noticed in computer simulations.
2. For more details on delays see Forrester (1969: 408–409).
3. Professor W. Weidlich has remarked upon the possibility of a transformation of the stable equilibrium to an unstable equilibrium after the introduction of information lags in the initial system and advised me to investigate this problem analytically. I agree with this valuable observation.

The Long Wave is the least understood
and most important (cycle) ...
but it moves so slowly that
the motion is imperceptible to the human eye.
Yet like the glaciers, it
can have the most devastating
effect on the countryside.

John Sterman (quoted from Prowse 1992: 28)

CHAPTER 5

THE PROFIT–WAGE SPIRAL

R. Solow has plotted a scatter graph of the employment rate and the relative wage for
the US non-farm business economy for 1947–86. He has come to a very interesting
conclusion from the crudest sort of comparison with data (Solow 1990: 39–40):

> If the [Goodwin] model were an exact description for that place and that period, the
> successive data points would parade clockwise around in a closed orbit. ... there *is*
> a suggestion of predominantly clockwise motion, but in three separate episodes. ...
> The displacements are quite large and they suggest that the Goodwin model cannot
> be the only mechanism governing the relation between the wage share and the
> employment rate. ... It would make more sense for me if the Goodwin mechanism
> were to apply on a time scale considerably longer than the ordinary business cycle.

This chapter is in line with this idea of the Nobel Prize winner.

5.1   A LIMIT CYCLE OF UNEVEN GROWTH

In the USA over the period 1790–1990 and in the UK during 1840–1990, the rates
of growth of the real per capita GNP have oscillated around the same 1.79% long-run
average annual rate. The main periods of expansion have alternated with prolonged periods
of recession and stagnation. The periods of economic hardship span over the 1830s and
1840s, the 1870s through to the late 1890s, the 1920s and 1930s, and the period from
about 1974 through to the beginning of the 1990s (see Mosekilde, Thomsen and Sterman
1991: 16).

There have been substantial fluctuations in the growth rates of the OECD economies
after the Second World War. For example, in the USA the average growth rate of GDP
was about 3.2% during 1948–90, in the 1950s 4%, the 1960s 4.1%, the 1970s 3.1%, the
1980s 2.7%, the 1990s 2.1%.[1] The Clinton administration "projects GDP growth over the
long term at roughly 2.4 percent per year — a figure consistent with the experience so
far during this business cycle as well as with reasonable growth rates of the economy's
supply-side components" (*Economic Report of the President* 1999: 83).

Over the period 1959–73 the real GNP per worker-hour grew 1.85% annually, over the period 1973–90 real GNP per worker-hour slowed to 0.73% per year and accelerated to 1.0% per year in 1990–97 (see Krugman and Lawrence 1994: 26; Weisskopf, Bowles and Gordon 1983: 410; Klinov 1998: 17). Still "with slower growth in the working-age population and slower trend productivity growth since the early 1970s, it is understandable that GDP has grown more slowly than it did in the 1960s" (*Economic Report of the President* 1999: 25–26). The main increases in unemployment have generally coincided with recessions. According to Sterman, the USA and other market economies have been in the decline phase of the post-war long wave since the 1970s (see Sterman 1992: 10).

The period 1948–73 is commonly referred to as the "long boom" or "golden age" among industrialised capitalist nations (see Table 5.1). The officially registered unemployment ratio in the OECD countries in the 1960s was lower than 3%, on average. The European Community had an unemployment rate of 10.4% and the USA a rate of 6.8% in 1993 (see Institut der deutschen Wirtschaft Köln 1994a: 44). The average unemployment rate in the USA for the year 1998 dropped to 4.5%, its lowest level since 1969, while in the European economic and monetary union (euro-zone) it was still above 10%.[2]

The "golden age" should be compared with the Great Depression. On the year-to-year base, the index of the real GNP slumped in the USA from 154.3 in 1929 to 108.6 in 1933, in Germany from 102.9 in 1928 to 79.6 in 1932 and in Austria from 105.1 in 1929 to 81.5 in 1933 (1913 = 100). The unemployment ratio rose during 1929–37 to 22.5% in Great Britain (1932), 25.9% in Austria (1933), 30.1% in Germany (1932) and 32.7% in 1936 in the Netherlands (see Butschek 1985: 42, 46). At the depth of the Great Depression in the USA, the unemployment rate was 25% in 1933 (Sterman, 1992: 28).

Marx was among the very first social scientists to take a long-term view on economic growth and fluctuations. He drew particular attention to the wavelike movement of the wheat prices during 1650–1859 and identified the periods of major rise and decline in prices for this commodity, unnoticed by Ricardo (see Marx 1978b: 153–154, 255). The lengths of these periods were about 50 years.

N. D. Kondratiev continued Marx's analysis. He analysed prices of major commodities, interest rates, industrial production, raw materials consumption and foreign trade. This Russian economist argued for the existence of a 50–60-year cyclical motion and saw its material base in the wearing out, replacement and extension of fixed capital.

Interest in the Kondratiev cycles has been rekindled with the beginning of the long-term recession trend in the capitalist economy after 1970. "The most important social reason for studying business cycles is to attempt the removal of the amount of unemployment created during recessions", the experts of *The Economist* write (see *The Economist* Newspaper Ltd 1982: 12). However, it remains disputable whether the long-wave pattern really determines GDP dynamics in the USA and other industrialised market economies.[3] The small number

Table 5.1 Economic performance of the UK and USA before and after 1973 (percentages)

	Growth of GDP per employed person		Change in GDP per capita			Unemployment	
	1960–73	1974–90	1790–1990	1960–73	1974–90	1960–73	1974–90
UK	2.9	1.5	1.79[a]	2.6	1.8	1.9	7.4
USA	2.0	0.6	1.79	2.7	1.5	4.8	6.9

[a]1840–1990 for the UK. *Sources:* Berry (1991: 67), and Kenworthy (1995: 7).

of long swings of economic activity in capitalist countries after the Industrial Revolution at the end of the eighteenth century in England is a factor of uncertainty for statistically testing the long-wave hypothesis. The earlier in history a statistical record was made, the more unsatisfactory the quality of respective data generally.

Another approach is chosen in this book. It can be shown that our model possesses a generic structure generating the long-period fluctuations and growth simultaneously. It mimics the persistence of cycles arising in feedback loops with alternating polarity.

The example of damping fluctuations with a period of about six years was provided in section 4.2.[4] The fluctuations are not strictly periodic. The amplitude and phasing of each variable are determined structurally. In a linear case all variables oscillate with the same frequency and damping, only their amplitudes and phasing differ, these being parameters fixed for each variable separately by extraneous factors or initial conditions (see Allen 1955: 161).

The values of variables in that example are far from being realistic. The following values better calibrate the model to historically reasonable magnitudes (see Table 5.2). We use vaguely plausible equilibrium values of the main variables, relying on international statistics and our predecessors.

The equilibrium wage share, 0.75, coincides with that of van der Ploeg (1983: 259). It is close to the employees' compensation share in national income in the USA: 75.9% in 1970, 76.9% in 1991 (see Institut der deutschen Wirtschaft Köln 1994a: 55). These magnitudes for the USA are calculated without taking into account changes in the share of employees in the total economically active population. The equilibrium employment ratio, 0.9, is identical with that of Goodwin (1990: 69, 87).

The equilibrium capital–output ratio, 4.17, is no more than a rough approximation of the Romer (1989) data for the USA (3.9) and Canada (3.7). Note that the capital coefficient, s, is calculated in our model as the ratio of fixed capital (net of depreciation) to net product, while it is calculated in the official statistics as the ratio of fixed assets to GDP. Some uncertainties in parameters remain.

Let us choose an initial magnitude of the rate of employment $v_0 = 0.89 \neq v_2$ without an initial displacement of other variables from their equilibrium values ($u_0 = u_2, s_0 = s_2$). Then a damping cyclical motion is obtained, the length of the cycle being approximately 60 years. Because the real parts of the eigenvalues are all negative, the fixed point E_2 is

Table 5.2 Examples of long waves

m_1	m_2	Steady-state growth rate $(\hat{a}_2, \hat{a}_e)$	Real eigen-value λ	Conjugate pair of eigenvalues $\alpha \pm \beta i$	Period of fluctuations in the linearised model (years)	Relative speed of convergence to E_2 or (or E_e) in the nonlinear model
0.02	0.5	0.04	−0.0043	−0.0039± 0.1077i	58.3	Low
0	1	0.04	–	−0.0135 ±0.1070i	58.7	Moderate

Notes:
1. The length of the fluctuations is about 60 years.
2. If $m_1 = 0.02$ and $m_2 = 0.5$ then the initial vector $(s_0, u_0, v_0) = (s_2, u_2, v_2 - 0.01) \approx (4.17, 0.75, 0.89)$. If $m_1 = 0$ and $m_2 = 1$, the model becomes two-dimensional. Then the initial vector $(u_0, v_0) = (u_2, v_2 - 0.01) \approx (0.75, 0.89)$ and $s_0 \approx 4.17$. The latter case is called degenerate.
3. The magnitudes of the other parameters: $n_1 = 0.01, n_2 = 0.04, r = 0.062, b = 0.1, g = 0.02, n = 0.02$.

a sink. Moreover, it is locally asymptotically stable. It is not implied that our illustrative constellations are in fact empirically accurate.

Thus our model generates damping long waves. Table 5.2 also displays the relative speed of convergence for different magnitudes of the two significant parameters. The capital–output ratio does not change in the degenerate, two-dimensional case that is given in the bottom row of this table. Figures 5.1 and 5.2 illustrate these experiments.

The introduction of a material delay (investment lag) in the equation for fixed capital formation (3.10) alters the dynamic properties of the trajectories. Diverging fluctuations arise if the delay is bigger than a certain critical magnitude, and it is necessary to change other parameters to retain stability. In particular, this material delay may be compensated by an increase in n_2.

For the above constellation of the other coefficients, inequality (3.37) turns into equality if $b_0 \approx 0.357 < m_2 = 0.5$. The new non-trivial fixed point corresponding to this critical magnitude (x^*) equals approximately (4.17, 0.75, 0.74). When b is increased from $b < b_0$ to $b > b_0$, the system (3.21)–(3.23) loses its local stability at x^* because the real part of the complex conjugate eigenvalues becomes positive (see Table 5.3). According to the Hopf bifurcation theorem (the existence part), there exist periodic solutions bifurcating from the new locally unstable fixed point at $b = b_0$.

I have simulated limit cycles in the phase space, which show the other possible pattern of long waves about the trend, using the software *Powersim* and *Gnans* (see Martensson 1993; Myrtveit 1995). In agreement with the Hopf theorem, numerical calculations do depict attraction of trajectories starting in the neighbourhood of x^* (at $b = b_0 \approx 0.357$) by different limit cycles. Figures 5.3, 5.4(a) and (b) depict time graphs for the state variables (data from Table 5.3).

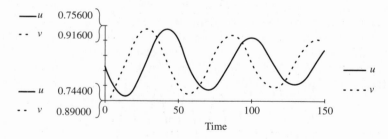

Figure 5.1   The converging long-period fluctuations generated by the three-dimensional model

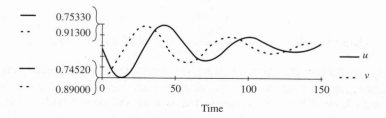

Figure 5.2   The long-period fluctuations in the degenerate case

Table 5.3   The example of the long wave

Steady-state growth rate $(\hat{a}_2)$	Real eigenvalue λ_3	Conjugate pair of eigenvalues λ_1 and λ_2 $\alpha \pm \beta i$	$\dfrac{d(\text{Re}\lambda_{1,2}(b))}{db}$ for $b = b_0$	Period of fluctuations in the linearised model (years)
0.04	-0.004	$0 \pm 0.098i$	0.075	64.127

Notes:
1. The length of the fluctuations is about 65 years.
2. $m_1 = 0.02$, $m_2 = 0.5$, $n_1 = 0.01$, $n_1 = 0.04$, $r = 0.062$, $b_0 = 0.5 - 1/7 \approx 0.357\,143$, $g = 0.02$, $n = 0.02$; the equilibrium vector $(s_2, u_2, v_2) \approx (4.1667, 0.75, 0.7373)$, the initial vector $(s_0, u_0, v_0) = (4.1667, 0.75, 0.89)$.
3. At $b = b_0$, $a_1 a_2, = a_0$, $(\lambda^2 + a_1)(\lambda + a_2) = 0$, $\lambda_{1,2} = \pm(-a_1)^{1/2} = \pm i[ru_2v_2(1/s_2 + n_2)]^{1/2}$, $\lambda_3 = (b_0 - m_2)n_2u_2$.

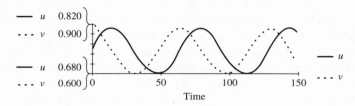

Figure 5.3   The long-wave pattern of the relative wage and employment ratio motion

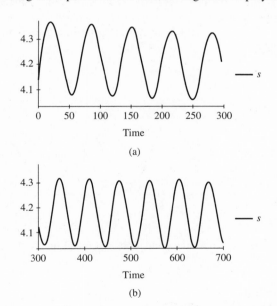

Figure 5.4   The long-wave pattern of the capital-output ratio motion

A picking up of a periodic attractor in a given time integration depends on the starting conditions (the initial values of s, v, u). In each such case the oscillations increase in amplitude until limited by nonlinearity in the system and persist within certain limits. Note that a similar multiplicity of alternative stable attracting solutions dependent on the starting conditions is typical of nonlinear driven oscillators (see Thompson 1987: 25).

5.2   THE PUZZLE OF UNEMPLOYMENT IN RETROSPECT[5]

Now we are well prepared to give an economic interpretation for the Hopf bifurcation via changes in the control parameter b. The initial Phillips equation corresponds to the simplest type of policy: $\hat{w}$ is made proportional to the excess of the employment ratio over its equilibrium, and r measures the strength of this policy.

If we look at the scatter graph of $\hat{w}$ and v on Figure 5.5, we will observe that there is a clear tendency for the rate of growth of the unit real wage to be high when unemployment is low and to be low when unemployment is high. Thus the model agrees with the first Phillips conjunction.

The second Phillips conjunction was about the relationship between the rate of change of money wages and the rate of change of the unemployment ratio (see Phillips 1958: 290). He argued that the latter variable typically produces a negative influence on the former: the higher the growth rate of employment, the higher the rate of change of money wages, other things being equal.

Let us look at any given level of unemployment in Figure 5.6. There is a distinct tendency for the rate of change of the unit real wage to be above the average for that

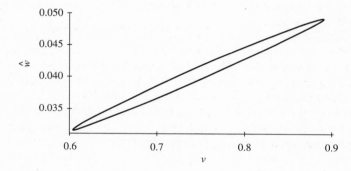

Figure 5.5   The employment ratio as the factor of the rate of change of real wage.
Counter-clockwise motion

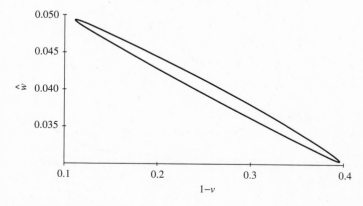

Figure 5.6   The unemployment ratio as a factor of the rate of change of real wage. Clockwise
motion

level of unemployment when unemployment is growing during the downswings of the long wave, and to be below the average for that level of unemployment when unemployment is decreasing during the upswings of the long wave. This result seemingly contradicts the second Phillips conjunction.

The results of our simulations and the Phillips findings for the relationship between unemployment and the rate of change of money wage rates in the UK (1861–1957) are not directly comparable since he has used data on the nominal wage. Still it is interesting that the loop direction for these variables in the five years from 1953 to 1957 coincides with ours.

Phillips (1958: 297) has put forward a hypothesis that this peculiarity of 1953–57 resulted from a time lag in the real adjustment of wage rates to the unemployment ratio and to the rate of change of this ratio. Such a time lag appeared as a result of institutional changes on the labour market after the Second World War. The importance of these changes has been demonstrated in section 4.3 in agreement with the Phillips idea.

R. Lipsey (1960) has found out that, on the average experiences of the 1922–57 period, times of falling unemployment were associated with lower rates of change of money wage rates than were times of rising unemployment. This finding contradicts the second Phillips conjunction and possibly supports ours. My reservation again reflects the differences between the dynamics of real and monetary wage rates that does not allow a straightforward validation.

Figure 5.7 adds details to the co-movement of these variables over phases of the long wave. When the rate of change of the unit real wage is average, the rate of change of employment is highest or lowest. The rate of change of the unit real wage, being greater than average, declines along with a decrease of the employment ratio during the recession. This rate, being lower than average, grows along with an increase in the employment ratio during the recovery of the long wave. The growth rates of the unit real wage are generally higher during the recession when the employment ratio decreases than during the recovery when the employment ratio increases. The growth rates of the unit real wage are generally lower during the depression when the employment ratio decreases than during the boom when the employment ratio increases.

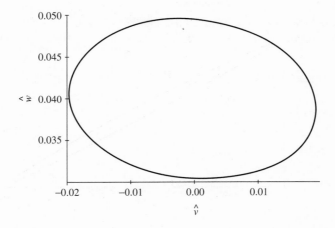

Figure 5.7   The rate of change of the employment ratio ($\hat{v}$) as a factor of the rate of change of unit real wage ($\hat{w}$). Counter-clockwise motion

Note that neither Phillips nor Lipsey included a profit rate as a factor of the wage rate in their models. Kaldor advised relating wage increases to the increase in profitability. He wrote (Kaldor 1959: 293): "The *bargaining strength* of labour is ... closely related to the prosperity of industry, which determines both the eagerness of labour unions to demand higher wages and the willingness and ability of employers to grant them."

What was right in 1959 for the recovery of the fourth Kondratiev cycle is also appropriate for the current expansion of the business cycle in the USA, based on the earlier investment-driven recovery from the recession and slow growth of the early 1990s. The US economy has had a lead over other developed market economies in overcoming the depression phase of the fourth Kondratiev cycle. It is not yet clear whether or not the USA have entered the recovery of the fifth wave.

Profitability and the rate of change of the unit real wage decline simultaneously during recession and increase together during recovery (see Figure 5.8). They move in opposite directions during boom and depression phases. Provided that $\hat{w} \neq 0$, we obtain the wage elasticity of demand for labour $\hat{L}/\hat{w}$. It follows from equations (3.5) and (3.13) that

$$\hat{L}/\hat{w} = [\hat{K} - (n_1 + n_2 u)]/[-g_1 + rv + g_2 + b(\hat{K}/L)]. \tag{5.1}$$

Figure 5.9 displays a scatter graph for the wage elasticity of demand for labour $\hat{L}/\hat{w}$ and profitability $\hat{K}$. The higher the profitability, the higher the elasticity. Besides profitability, elasticity is apparently positively correlated with the rate of change of profitability, as times of falling profitability are associated with a lower elasticity than times of rising profitability.

Figure 5.10 shows a scatter graph for the wage elasticity of demand for labour and the labour share. Elasticity is negatively correlated with the labour share and the rate of change of this share. At the steady state

$$\hat{L}_2/\hat{w}_2 = n/(n_1 + n_2 u_2) = n(1 - m_2)/m_1. \tag{5.2}$$

The higher the equilibrium relative wage, the lower the wage elasticity of demand for labour. This conclusion is in agreement with neo-classical theory, although the latter defines the equilibrium labour share as $1 - m_2$ that typically differs from u_2 in our model (see Saint-Paul 1996: 291).

Let us turn our attention once more to the modified Phillips equation (3.13). I believe that the proposed modification absorbs true aspects of the different views on factors of

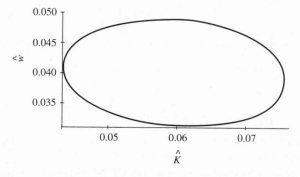

Figure 5.8   A profit–wage spiral. Counter-clockwise motion

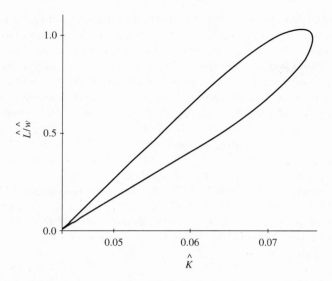

Figure 5.9   Profitability as the factor of wage elasticity of demand for labour. Clockwise motion

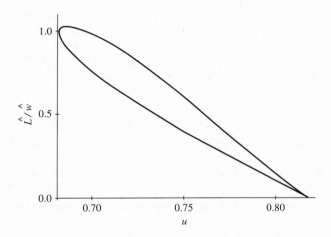

Figure 5.10   Relative wage as the factor of wage elasticity of demand for labour.
Counter-clockwise motion

the rate of change of the unit real wage. The equation can be transformed into

$$\hat{w} = -g_1 + rv + g_2 + b(\hat{K/L})$$
$$= -g + rv + b\hat{K} - b\hat{L}$$
$$= -g + rv + b(1 - u)/s - b\hat{v} - bn. \tag{5.3}$$

Note that the Phillips variables v and $\hat{v}$ are preserved. Lipsey would be satisfied with the sign of the term $b\hat{v}$ in this equation. Kaldor would appreciate the enforcing term $b(1 - u)/s$ on the right-hand side of this equation. This result has surprised me because I conceived the idea of modifying the Phillips equation on the other ground (see section 3.3).

The two enforcing terms rv and $b(1-u)/s$ bring about the potent movements of the state variables near x^*. The system (3.21)–(3.23) loses its local stability at some critical b ($b_0 \approx 0.357$, in our example). The term $(-b\hat{v})$ is a drag on the amplitude of fluctuations.

Such a corrective action is a special case of a *derivative* control that has been added to the Phillips equation. As $\hat{v}$ is a leading indicator of the cyclical movement in relation to $\hat{v}$, this derivative control has a somewhat similar effect to that which would be obtained by basing the corrective action on a forecast of a demand for labour power (cf. Phillips 1962: 7). In fact, we face here the feed-forward, or anticipatory, control *in embryo*. Its more rife forms will be introduced in Chapter 6.

Let us examine what will happen after removing the term $b\hat{v}$ from the right-hand side of equation (5.3). Our modification affects equation (3.23), whereas equations (3.21) and (3.22) remain untouched. The modified system has the same unstable equilibrium E_2, but without a limit cycle in the vicinity. Numerical runs show that owing to very strong fluctuations the state variables leave the permissible region and the system terminates.

The Lie derivative calculated for stable limit cycles for initial points sufficiently close to the fixed-point equilibrium is negative, thus indicating that the dissipative property of the initial system is retained. A further increase of b over b_0 brings about diverging fluctuations without visibly transiting to a chaotic attractor. In other words, due to nonlinearity in the system, a substantial increase of b over b_0 destabilises the system.

At the limit cycles the maximum of v corresponds to the minimum of s and vice versa, while $u = u_2$. It is more difficult to find out what correspondence exists between $\hat{P}$ and v at a closed orbit. Recall that $\hat{P} = \hat{a} + \hat{v} + n$, where $\hat{a}$ is greatest at u_{max}, when $v = v_2 < v_{max}.\hat{v}$ is highest at $u = u_{min}$. The following transformation may be helpful in answering this question:

$$\hat{P} = \hat{a} + \hat{v} + n$$
$$= m_1 + m_2(n_1 + n_2 u) + (1 - u)/s - (n_1 + n_2 u) + n - n$$
$$= m_1 + (1 - u)/s - (1 - m_2)(n_1 + n_2 u). \tag{5.4}$$

The minimal or maximal u is attainable at $v = v_2$, when $s = s_2 < s_{max}$. The changes in s are less important for the dynamics of $\hat{P}$ than those of u in our example. We may conclude that $\hat{P}_{max}$ and $\hat{P}_{min}$ are achievable in the vicinity of $v = v_2 < 1$. Figure 5.11 illustrates this conclusion.

Let us return to the Okun law that explains unemployment by co-movement in output only (see Okun 1962; also section 3.4). We see that two different levels of the employment

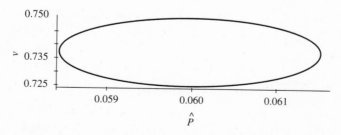

Figure 5.11   The relationship between the rate of economic growth and employment ratio. Counter-clockwise motion

ratio correspond to each magnitude of the rate of economic growth in the interval $(\hat{P}_{min}, \hat{P}_{max})$. So this Okun law may be only partially true.

It is not clear whether the self-regulation in the extended model could be supported by another kind of proportional control, i.e. by policies designed gradually to raise the equilibrium level v_2 from 0.9 to any desired and feasible level of v, say 0.98. This question remains open, especially in the context of globalisation.

R. Goodwin (1990: 110) argued that these policies would require tight discipline from employers and employees, their readiness to forgo raising real wages in consequences of the tightness of the labour market, planning in advance of government expenditures and effective implementing of such a programme. In the first half of the 1990s, trade unions in Germany, Great Britain and other OECD countries have been showing increasing willingness to forgo higher pay in order to retain jobs.

However, a reduction of the share of GDP going to investment by one-third in the EU between the mid-1970s and 1997 brought about the rise of the unemployment ratio from 3% in the 1960s and early 1970s to 11 percent (see Modigliani and La Malfa 1998). The model explains why a return to the EU level of unemployment of the 1960s is hardly possible without the recovery of investment to corresponding levels. The formula (3.17) and Figures 5.12 and 5.13 support this association.

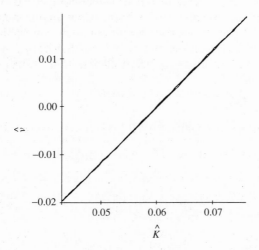

Figure 5.12   The rate of capital accumulation ($\hat{K}$) as a factor of the rate of change of employment ratio ($\hat{v}$)

Figure 5.13   The rate of change of capital–output ratio ($\hat{s}$) as a factor of the rate of change of employment ratio ($\hat{v}$)

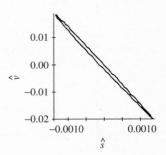

The growth rate of the employment ratio depends on the growth rate of capital stock and the rate of change of the capital–output ratio. Thus, an economic policy for reducing unemployment would imply a revival of investment and an improvement in capital productivity.

Let us now look at West German statistics. The share of employees' compensation in national income, adjusted for structural changes in the economically active population, has decreased since 1982 to the level of 1960 (from 72.5 to 65% in 1990). The 1970 share of employees in the economically active population is taken in these calculations for the whole period. The rate of unemployment has grown from 3.8% in 1980 to 8.2% in 1993.[6] The growth rate of labour productivity has surpassed that of the unit real wage.[7] The rate of change of the participation rate has become negative (-1.0% per annum) in 1980–93 compared with 0.5% per annum in 1970–80 (see Table 3.2).

The USA have experienced a similar process. G. Duménil and D. Lévy (1993) have found a clear indication of rising profitability in the USA in the 1980s after its decline in the 1970s.[8] In the view of Bowles, Gordon and Weisskopf, (1986, 1989), the tight monetary policies and severe recessions of the early 1980s were calculated attempts by a conservative administration to restore aggregate profit rates.

Declining and stagnating wages of the average American worker in these years may be considered as a contributory factor for a real technology pay-off for investors. The rate of change of real wages and salaries had averaged 1.6% a year from 1960 to 1973. It was -0.7% a year during 1978–86, on average. Measured as average hourly earnings in the private non-agricultural sector for production or non-supervisory employees, average real wages had fallen since 1972 and stood below their value in 1968.[9]

Table 5.1 posts the growth in the average rate of unemployment after 1973. The rate of growth of the participation rate declined in 1980–93 to zero compared with 1.3% per annum in 1970–80 (see Table 3.2).

Bhaskar and Glyn's (1995) study of the investment trends suggested that declining profitability accounted for a major part of the investment slowdown in the major OECD countries after 1973. Profitability recovery was strongest in the 1980s in those countries where unemployment rose most and labour cost competitiveness improved. The crucial difference for profitability between the 1980s and 1973–79 lay in the slower growth of real wages. The cut of two-thirds in real wage growth more than accounts for the reversal in the trend of the wage share from increase to decrease.

Glyn (1997: 608) concludes: "the fairly robust correlation between rising unemployment and restored manufacturing profitability confirms that differences in the unemployment rate across countries do indicate the pressures exerted in the labour market by the reserve army of labour. These evidently have the impact on the profit rate described by the classical economists."

My model explains fairly well these connections between the growth rate of the unit real wage, unemployment ratio, profitability and labour share in the net national product. In their turn, they also support this model empirically at least in what concerns the basic patterns of behaviour at the macro-level.

5.3   THE PHASES OF THE LONG WAVE

We have already seen that rapid productivity growth tends to go hand in hand with rapid output growth over the long term. The long wave imposes a more complicated relationship

Table 5.4   Indicators of the long wave

Phase end/ beginning	Growth rates of		Ratios	
	Output	Unit real wage	Labour bill share in the net output	The employment ratio
Recovery/boom	Maximal	Average	Minimal	Average
Boom/recession	Average	Maximal	Average	Maximal
Recession/depression	Minimal	Average	Maximal	Average
Depression/ recovery	Average	Minimal	Average	Minimal

between these rates and other variables. Note that in our numerical experiments production and employment have been expanded during all phases of the long wave. The latter has manifested itself in fluctuations of the growth rates of the macroeconomic variables, in particular.

I will identify four phases of a long wave — boom (prosperity), recession, depression and recovery — in the time series generated by the model (see Table 5.4). The latter emphasises growing labour unemployment and rising capital–output ratio during down-swings. This emphasis is also apparent in Ch. Freeman's theory of the long wave.

A more detailed picture is as follows.

Phase 1 (Recovery)

The labour bill share falls from its average magnitude to its minimum; the employment ratio grows from its minimum to the average level; the capital–output ratio falls from its maximum to the average magnitude; profitability increases from its average level to the maximum. The rise of the unit real wage does not interfere with the progress of accumulation and new employment generation.

Phase 2 (Boom)

The labour bill share increases from its minimum to its average value; as output growth is greater than productivity growth, the employment ratio grows from its average level to the maximum; the capital–output ratio moves from its average magnitude to its minimum; profitability falls from its maximum to the average level. "Accumulation slackens in consequence of the rise in price of labour, because the stimulus of gain is blunted" (Marx 1978a: 580). The model is in agreement with Marx's idea that "crises are always prepared by precisely a period in which wages rise generally and the working-class actually gets a larger share of that part of the annual product which is intended for consumption." (Marx 1978b: 415).

Phase 3 (Recession)

The labour bill share grows from its average magnitude to its maximum value; the employ-ment ratio decreases from its maximum to the average level; the capital–output ratio moves from its minimum to the average magnitude; profitability falls from its average level to the minimum. The greater relative overpopulation is the consequence of the lower rate of profit and the higher relative wage. Increasing unemployment is due to a growing mismatch between productivity growth and the reduced rate of growth in output (demand).

A competitive struggle among capitalists intensifies due to the fall in the rate of profit, causing a further temporary rise in the wage growth rate and a resultant temporary fall of the rate of profit (cf. Marx 1978c: 256). Chris Trinder, of the Public Finance Foundation in the UK, says: "To put it in a rather stylised way, there are companies where half the workers are losing their jobs and the other half are virtually doubling their pay. That is bad for employment and bad for the economy as a whole (*The Financial Times* 13 April 1993: 13). The growing capital intensity also fosters increases in the wage rate that tend to slow capital accumulation.

The rate of accumulation lessens; but with its lessening, the primary cause of that lessening (the excess of u over u_2) vanishes during the next phase. "The mechanism of ... capitalist production removes the very obstacles that it temporarily creates" (Marx 1978a: 580–581; see also Marx 1978b: 189). This is the starting point of large new investments.

Phase 4 (Depression)

The labour bill share decreases from its maximum magnitude to its average value; the employment ratio decreases from its average level to the minimum; the capital–output ratio moves from its average magnitude to its maximum; profitability rises from its minimum to the average level. The depression constitutes a structural crisis.

Substituting labour by capital and destroying employment (and workers' bargaining power) help to restore profitability during the depression via the painful and conflict-ridden process that in practice leads to structural unemployment. Governments can help to overcome the depression phase via a sound economic policy. However, government intervention has not been modelled.

The growth rate of the unit real wage ($\hat{w}$) is minimal at the beginning of the recovery phase, when the employment ratio is near its minimum and the rate of growth of capital intensity decreases below its average magnitude. The growth rate of the unit real wage ($\hat{w}$) is maximal at the beginning of the recession phase, when the employment ratio is near its maximum and the rate of growth of capital intensity increases over its average magnitude. In view of technological progress, a growing employment ratio does not necessarily require a reduction in the unit real wage in order to restore profitability.

The model does not treat unemployed persons' consumption explicitly. So it is reasonable also to calculate the rate of growth of real income per head as $\hat{w} + \hat{v}$. With the beginning of a recession, the model economy continues to grow in real terms, yet compared with the historic long-term trend the economy starts to decline (see Figure 5.14).

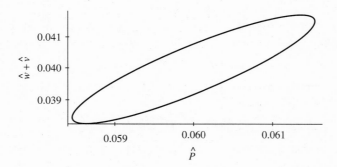

Figure 5.14   The rate of growth of real income per head and rate of growth of output.
Counter-clockwise motion

Rates of growth of real income per head decline during the downswing of the long wave. They increase during the upswing mostly due to the lower unemployment ratio.

The natural rate of growth is higher than warranted and actual rates during recessions and depressions, and is lower than that during recoveries and booms. The actual and warranted rates are very close to each other in our example. For the long wave, deviations between these rates are born, amplified to a certain maximal level and then eliminated in a periodical manner (see Figures 5.15 and 5.16). Notice that this is achieved without recourse to such instruments as an interest rate or a budget deficit.

The rates of growth of labour productivity and of the capital–output ratio are dependent upon the flow of new technological ideas and upon diffusion of innovations brought about by capital accumulation. In particular, the capital–output ratio tends to decrease in periods of accelerated growth (during the recovery and boom phases) fostering the rate of capital accumulation, and vice versa.

Van der Ploeg (1987: 11) writes: "The beauty of Goodwin-type models of cyclical growth is that they are able to explain short-run fluctuations around a long-run balanced growth trajectory." We have seen that they may explain long-run fluctuations as well. The model shows the clear economic mechanism that causes the system to move upward from its lower turning point and downward from its upper turning point. The reader may be well informed that an endogenous explanation of turning points of the long wave has been a stumbling block for many theoreticians in this field of science.

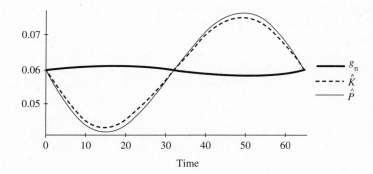

Figure 5.15   The natural, actual and warranted rates of growth $(g_n, \hat{P}, \hat{K})$

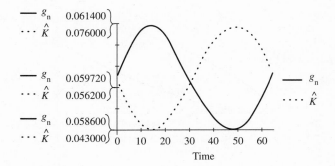

Figure 5.16   The natural and warranted rates of growth $(g_n, \hat{K})$. The normalised view

The most important result of the boom phase is relative over-accumulation of capital. Marx (1978c: 255–256) writes: "It is over-production of means of production only in so far as the latter *serve as capital*. ... It is no contradiction that this over-production of capital is accompanied by more or less considerable relative over-population."

Profitability and growth are at their nadir in the phase transition from recession to depression. Many firms experience bankruptcies because of declining profits at the same time. At the end of the depression profitability is at its average value; when profitability is greatest (the beginning of the boom phase) employment is average. The improving profitability is engendering a too speedy expansion of output and employment, thus favouring labour's bargaining power and its share in national income, which could be only partially offset (in our example) by the drop of the capital–output coefficient during the boom phase.

Growing labour productivity (with decreasing capital–output ratio) enables the simultaneous growth of employment and of the profit rate during recoveries and the simultaneous growth of employment and of the labour bill share during booms. Unit real wages must fall in relation to productivity during depressions and recoveries (but not necessarily in absolute terms) in order to restore profitability (cf. Marx 1978a: 582). Contrary to the Ricardo–Marx law of the rate of profit to fall and in agreement with Marx's reservations concerning this tendency, our model shows that the rate of profit grows during the depression and recovery phases of the long wave.

Menshikov and Klimenko (1985) have produced long-term data for the USA that support the hypothesis of a long-wave pattern in average industrial profit rates, and they are consistent with Kleinknecht's data for West German manufacturing industry (Kleinknecht 1987: 216–236).

5.4   PRODUCTIVITY, PROFITABILITY AND THE SCALE EFFECT

In the model economy, technical progress and growth of the labour force tend to result in steady economic growth, while the long waves could represent important fluctuations about this trend, lasting some 60–65 years. Such a long-wave pattern of economic growth is determined by the internal structure of capital accumulation displayed above within a very stylised institutional setting.

For this setting, the high technological dynamism benefits both classes and mitigates social contradictions in the process of income distribution. I believe the reader will agree with the idea that "stimulating the technical dynamism of the economy (*raising* the technical progress function) ... is not only (or perhaps mainly) a matter of more scientific education and more expenditure on research, but of higher quality of business management which is more alert in searching for technical improvements and less resistant to their introduction" (Kaldor and Mirrles 1962: 190).

Our analytical findings and simulation experiments support the conclusion that "no intrinsic clustering of innovations is necessary to produce long period fluctuations of economic activity" (Silverberg and Lehnert 1992: 17). The flow of invention and innovation is itself contingent upon the rate of capital accumulation. It is shown that the model is consistent with Kaldor's prominent stylised facts. This model could be transformed into an optimal control model. Then an interesting question arises whether an optimal (cyclical) strategy exists that can give rise to the stable limit cycle in the optimal control model.[10] Introduction of a material delay in the equation for the fixed capital formation

(3.10) destroys the limit cycles. The problem of their existence in the extended model deserves special research.

The model predicts that during the depression and recovery phases the rate of growth of productivity declines ($\hat{a}$) while the capital growth rate and profitability ($\hat{K}$) increase, mostly because the relative wage decreases. The average unit real wage and real income per head can also fall.

Marx (1978d: 18) pointed out that entrepreneurs must more often resort to innovations in the periods when profit sinks to a level which is lower than normal. In our basal model, when the profitability (warranted rate of economic growth) is lowest at the end of the recession phase, the rate of change of labour productivity is highest (see Figure 5.17). How do we explain it?

The following interpretation suggests itself. The innovations induced by income distribution then exert a strong positive influence on profitability as if they occurred in clusters. Thus the technological breakthrough in the model is the reaction of entrepreneurs to the downturn. If it is true, then this property of the outlined theory incorporates Schumpeter's and G. Mensch's view that the clustering of innovations causes the Kondratiev cycles. The difference is that such a clustering becomes endogenous instead of being exogenous.

However, this interpretation in favour of the model is not yet indisputable. Innovations should, of course, materialise in new investments before they can effect the growth of labour productivity. It first requires investment in capital goods industries, a process that can feed on itself for decades. "The process of rebuilding necessarily causes the economy to overshoot the long-run needs of replacement of depreciated assets and long-run growth", Sterman (1992: 7) argues. Our gaming experiments in Chapter 2 support this point of view.

It is logical to expect that a maximal growth rate of labour productivity happens later than predicted by our basal model. This delay does appear after the introduction of a scale effect together with a new element of competition between workers below.

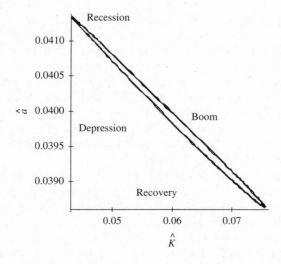

Figure 5.17   Profitability ($\hat{K}$) as the factor of the rate of growth of labour productivity ($\hat{a}$). Counter-clockwise motion with a period of about 65 years in the basal model

The long-term dynamics of capital goods industries, excess capacities and self-ordering of durable assets are not treated explicitly in our model of the long wave. This limitation is made to highlight endogenous technological progress that is not the focus of the Sterman model. I believe that the unified theory of the long wave should include strong elements of both models.

The motion of labour productivity and technical composition of capital (capital intensity) is synchronous in our model with that of the relative wage, since the relationships between $\hat{a}$, K/L and u are linear and positive. This rather simple and doubtful pattern of motion is, in my view, additional indirect evidence that there exist factors which affect these variables but have not yet been included in the model.

It follows from equations (3.4) and (3.5) that the growth rate of labour productivity changes according to the formula

$$\hat{a} = m_1 + m_2(n_1 + n_2 u).$$

It is clear that the higher u is, the greater is $\hat{a}$. So the model generates an accelerated productivity growth during the boom and recession of the long wave. This property is hardly empirically valid. Moreover, the growth of the employment ratio near E_2 during a recovery is promoted by a decelerating growth of labour productivity (see Figure 5.18).

There is an argument against trying to preserve jobs by curbing productivity growth: "The reason for this is that rapid productivity growth tends to go hand in hand with rapid output growth. In the 1960s, when productivity in OECD economies grew more than twice as fast as it has over the past decade, unemployment remained low. Only in the 1970s, when the growth in productivity (and in output) slumped, did unemployment rise" (*The Economist* 1995, 337 (7942): 21–22).

This problem of disparity between the pattern of behaviour generated by the model and the apparent development could be at least partially solved if we also take into account that a growth of labour productivity is retarded by a slowdown in output because of the scale effect that was dealt with in Chapter 1. A modified technical progress function is now

$$\hat{a} = m_1 + m_2(K/L) + m_3 \hat{v}, \quad m_1 \geq 0, \, 1 \geq m_2 \geq 0, \, m_3 \geq 0. \tag{3.4'}$$

Increases in the employment ratio also facilitate labour productivity gains in this equation.

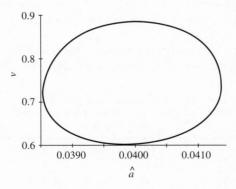

Figure 5.18   The employment ratio (v) versus the growth rate of labour productivity ($\hat{a}$) in the basal model. Clockwise motion

This augmentation — positive feedback between a production (demand) gain and increasing labour productivity — destabilises cyclical growth. Simulations which are skipped here have demonstrated diverging fluctuation in the phase space for different reasonable constellations of parameters.

My hypothesis is that the "intra-specific" competition among employees is a balancing factor. It is already reflected in the equation for the relative wage but not in the equation for the employment ratio in the basal model. The employment ratio affects capital intensity positively in an extended mechanisation (automation) function:

$$(\hat{K/L}) = n_4 + n_2 u + n_3 v = n_1 + n_2 u + n_3 v - n_3 v_2 = n_1 + n_2 u + n_3 (v - v_2),$$

$$n_4 = n_1 - n_3 v_2, n_2 \geq 0, n_3 \geq 0. \tag{3.5'}$$

It can be easily shown that these two modifications do not change the equilibrium E_2 but can affect its stability. The latter now depends also on the new control parameters m_3 and n_3.

Paradoxically, the efforts that stabilise cyclical growth strongly facilitate the scale effect instead of dampening it! The crux of the matter is shown by transforming (3.4') with the help of (3.5'):

$$\hat{a} = m_1 + m_2(\hat{K/L}) + m_3 \hat{v}$$

$$= m_1 + m_2(n_1 + n_2 u + n_3(v - v_2)) + m_3 \hat{v}$$

$$= m_1 + m_2(n_1 + n_2 u) + m_2 n_3(v - v_2) + m_3 \hat{v}.$$

The total scale effect equals the sum of $m_2 n_3(v - v_2)$ and $m_3 \hat{v}$.

These modifications could be helpful to explain why the labour productivity slowdown may happen during the boom and recession phases of the long wave: although a growing relative wage promotes productivity growth as it does in the basal model, the scale effect can outbalance this positive influence in the model economy. This association reminds us of the real productivity slowdown in the USA that started when there was still the boom of the "golden age" mentioned at the beginning of this chapter (see also Table 5.5). Figure 5.19 illustrates co-movements of output and labour productivity.

An acceleration of the growth of labour productivity during the late depression brings about a delayed increment of the employment ratio above the minimum during the recovery in the extended model (see Figure 5.20), whereas in the basal model a similar increase in the employment ratio is accompanied by decelerating growth of labour productivity.

The inclusion of scale and competition effects has modified the connection between the growth rate of labour productivity and profitability: they do not move in opposite

Table 5.5 The average real growth rates of
GDP and GDP per working-hour in the USA
(% per year)

Period	GDP	GDP per working-hour
1961–73	4.1	2.6
1974–89	2.7	1.3
1990–97	2.2	1.0

Source: Klinov (1998: 17).

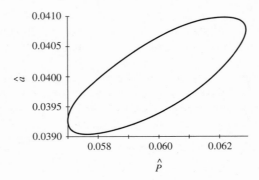

Figure 5.19   The scale effect of the production growth ($\hat{P}$) on the growth of labour productivity ($\hat{a}$) in the extended model. Counter-clockwise motion

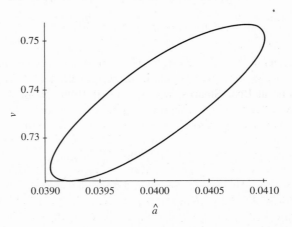

Figure 5.20   The employment ratio (v) versus the rate of growth of labour productivity ($\hat{a}$) in the extended model. Counter-clockwise motion

phases any more; improvements in profitability are the key for accelerating increases of labour productivity, worsening profitability paves the way for a slowdown of productivity growth. It appears to be realistic for the fourth Kondratiev cycle (Figure 5.21).

The following data are the input for the displayed computer simulations based on the extended model: $s_0 = 4.16667$, $u_0 = 0.75$, $v_0 = 0.75$; $b = 0.357$, $g = 0.02$, $m_1 = 0.02$, $m_2 = 0.5$, $m_3 = 0.3$, $n = 0.02$, $n_1 = 0.01$, $n_2 = 0.04$, $n_3 = 0.1098$, $r = 0.062$. For these magnitudes, I obtained experimentally the closed orbits displayed with a period of about 64.5 years. A slight decrease in n_3 yields diverging fluctuations, its slight increase produces converging fluctuations.

The simulated rates of profit and rates of change of productivity do not exhibit the same variability that we can deduce from the real data in an advanced capitalist economy. This implies a search for more intricate non-linearity.

We have already taken into account that the economy achieves substantial productivity gains in periods when demand for labour power expands especially rapidly. Still there is likely a weakening influence of each additional infinitesimal increment of the growth rate of the employment ratio on the growth rate of labour productivity.

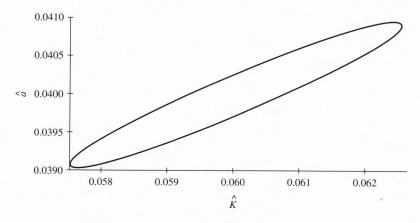

Figure 5.21   The growth of labour productivity ($\hat{a}$) versus profitability ($\hat{K}$) in the extended model. Counter-clockwise motion

In reality, major technological and productivity improvements take place during expansionary phases of a long wave. Mr Angell, a former governor of the Federal Reserve and now chief economist at Bear Stearns, writes (Angell 1999) about the current long-term recovery in the USA: "Technology-enhanced capital can substitute for labour and thereby add a stream of labour market re-entrants to an expanding economy. This explains how business fixed capital investment has risen to 13% of gross domestic product from 9%, driving the economy growth rate up to a stable 4% annual rate ... combining with low unemployment and even lower inflation. And, of course, consumer spending is pulled along with the faster growth rate, but remains at its customary 67% of GDP."

A slower expansion of employment, first, and decelerated productivity growth, second, indicates a maturing of a national technological system during a boom. A growth of productivity starts to decelerate when capital plant reaches the point of diminishing returns and this deceleration can become especially severe during a recession.

For presenting this stylised behavioural pattern, a particular functional form of a technical progress function is chosen:

$$\hat{a} = m_1 + m_2(\hat{K/L}) + m_3 \text{SIGN}(\hat{v})\text{ABS}(\hat{v})^\wedge j, \ m_1 \geq 0, \ 1 \geq m_2 \geq 0, \ m_3 \geq 0, \qquad (3.4'')$$

where $0 < j \leq 1$.

The POWERSIM built-in functions are used in this definition: ABS(x) is absolute value of x that is non-negative, $x^\wedge j$ is x raised to the j-th power, SIGN(x) is a sign of x. This modification produces no influence on the steady state $E_2 = (s_2, v_2, u_2)$ defined in section 3.5. The equation (3.4'') generalises the equations (3.4') and (3.4). Notice that the power j is the new control parameter of the model economy.

I have used in a simulation run new magnitudes of j (0.5), m_3 (0.05) and n_3 (0.25) as well as the same initial values of the variables and parameters of the previous simulation run reflected on Figure 5.21 ($s_0 = 4.16667$, $u_0 = 0.75$, $v_0 = 0.75$; $b = 0.357$, $g = 0.02$, $m_1 = 0.02$, $m_2 = 0.5$, $n = 0.02$, $n_1 = 0.01$, $n_2 = 0.04$, $r = 0.062$). For this constellation, the numerical experiment generates a seemingly stable limit cycle with a period about 68.5 years (see Figure 5.22).[11]

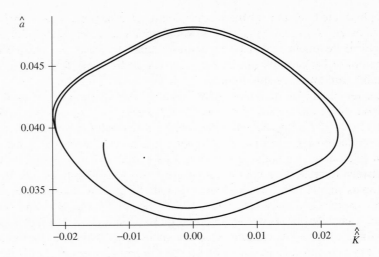

Figure 5.22   The growth of labour productivity ($\hat{a}$) versus the rate of change of profitability ($\hat{\hat{K}}$) in the model with the equation (3.4″). Counter-clockwise motion

Variability of the growth rates of labour productivity is higher in this experiment than observed in the previous simulation runs due to the new specification of the technical progress function. Another experiment has shown that there is a movement without oscillations to a vicinity of the fixed point, $E_2 = (s_2, v_2, u_2)$, if the total scale effect equals $m_2 n_3 (v - v_2)$ (for $m_3 = 0$).

The maximal (minimal) profitability is correlated in our model now with the fastest (slowest) growth of labour productivity. For the same profitability, the rate of change of labour productivity is higher when the profitability is growing than when profitability is declining. To my knowledge, the System Dynamics National Model of the MIT Sloan School of Management presented the respective linkages likewise (see Forrester 1993). We will return to this issue of variable returns in section 6.2.

5.5   CONCRETISING THE MODELS OF CYCLICAL GROWTH: DIFFERENT GATEWAYS

The highly irregular interaction of the long wave with shorter cycles has not yet been imitated with the help of the above models. I agree with my colleagues that "if the economy were linear, these different modes could evolve independently of one another, and their underlying courses could be studied separately. However, there is strong empirical and theoretical evidence to suggest that non-linear interaction between the various modes plays a critical role in determining the overall behaviour of the macroeconomic system" (Mosekilde, Thomsen and Sterman 1991: 18).

An interaction of different cyclical modes can produce deterministic chaos and other forms of complex dynamic phenomena. It is shown, in particular, how nonlinear dynamic phenomena arise in a model of the economic long wave when subjected to an external sinusoidal force, representing the coupling to other macroeconomic cycles (see Mosekilde, Thomsen and Sterman 1991).

More sophisticated versions of the models could use a parameter for a variable utilisation of fixed assets. As a result the models would get an additional flexibility and realism. Their analytical treatment would be far more complicated, alas. So the present models are a compromise between the desire for a greater realism and the need to contain the dimensionality within reasonable limits.

The other remaining shortcoming of my models is the assumption of homogeneity of factors (labour force and means of production). I accept the suggestion of the experts of the OECD (1991: 137), who believe that in order to measure the effect of technological change on productivity growth more accurately, it is necessary to keep track of different vintages of fixed assets embodying different levels of knowledge, explicitly considering the link between the rate of technological progress and scrapping rates. The measurement of labour inputs should reflect changes over time in the average number of hours worked, and possibly capture qualitative attributes of the workforce (education and skill levels).

The models included in this book are based on the assumption that the qualification of the labour force corresponds to technological requirements. This premise has enabled me to show that even in this idealised case involuntary unemployment could not be eliminated in the capitalist economy. Abandoning this premise would give rise to different categories of the relative surplus population, including the "stagnant".[12] The real processes of secular skill upgrading through education, training and learning-by-doing, on the one hand, and the obsolescence of skills acquired in the former phases of technological advance, on the other, should be explicitly reflected in further research.

Voluntary learning which may alter structure, delays and amplifications should be incorporated in the Goodwin-like model(s) as well. With the assistance of the elaborated approach one can test the consequences of alternative modes of paying workers over the business cycle in a "wage economy" (considered above) and in a "share economy" where workers are paid in part via profit or revenue sharing. More interesting lag distribution can be explored, etc. According to Richard Goodwin, one could also profitably investigate the effects of various types of policies pursued by workers, employers and state.[13]

Money supply, credit and the interest rate(s), money wage formation and price setting can be introduced as well. It is not yet clear whether a hybrid model of the business cycle(s) or a system of models interacting with each other would better implement these suggestions. One of the prospective directions for further investigations could be the study of instability as a moment of evolution towards a higher socio-economic order (see Chapter 6).

Following the principles of scientific abstraction, the factors initially disregarded are to be taken into account in order to strengthen the relevance of the model to the real world. A choice of additional factors are determined by the purpose of research. The eco-wave is rising at the gate.

NOTES

1. *The Financial Times*, 17 March 1993: 16; my own calculations of the geometrical means for the 1970s, 1980s and 1990–97 (for the 1990s) are based on the *Economic Report of the President* (1999: 328).
2. *Economic Report of the President* (1999: 43), redefining the unemployment rate to include discouraged workers as unemployed "increases the unemployment rate by no more than 0.4 percentage point" (ibid., p. 101); The Euro Indicators. Luxemburg: Eurostat, 16 April 1999.

3. In my opinion, the Council of Economic Advisers of the US President implicitly acknowledges the relevance of long cycles for the development of capitalism. They write: "Although the US economy has continued to experience fluctuations in output and employment in the more than half a century since then, it has avoided anything like the prolonged contraction of 1873–79, or the 30 percent contraction in output and 25 percent unemployment rate of the Great Depression" (*Economic Report of the President* 1999: 21). The comparison of the same phase of the successive Kondratiev cycles speaks for itself, doesn't it?
4. Professor R. Goodwin has pointed out that the cycle length of six years should, if possible, be altered by parameter changes: it is too long for the short cycle and not long enough for the major cycle in capitalist systems.
5. See Ryzhenkov (1998b).
6. These data are from Institut der deutschen Wirtschaft Köln (1994b: 28, 40; 1997: 21).
7. See *Die Zeit*, No. 41, 8 October 1993, p. 21.
8. See also the *Journal of Economic Literature*, December 1994, Vol. XXXII, No. 4: 1930–1931.
9. These data are from the *Economic Report of the President* (1988: 298).
10. A similar issue has been raised in Feichtinger, Novak and Wirl (1994).
11. The problem of orbital stability of the periodic oscillations requires a special treatment that goes beyond the scope of this book. See the theory of orbital stability, for example, in Šiljak 1969.
12. The stagnant reserve army is a part of the labour force with extremely irregular employment. It may not be completely covered by official statistics that count as unemployed those people who are actively looking for work, not those who have given up looking.
13. The author is grateful to Professor R. Goodwin for these hints.

Where Do We Come From?
What Are We?
Where Are We Going?

Paul Gauguin (1897)[1]

CHAPTER 6

THE EMERGING ECO-WAVE

This chapter is a step in ascending from the abstract to the concrete through one of the most promising gateways. The previous pages contain the equations of motion for the closed capitalist economy not constrained by natural resources. An extended model constructed in this chapter reflects the impact of economic activities upon natural environmental conditions. These conditions, in their turn, influence the growth rates of labour productivity and capital intensity. A policy, based on a perception of resource scarcity and pollution levels, is also included in this model. The steady states of the initial and extended models are compared (see Ryzhenkov 1998a, 1999). The model shows the adverse effects of social myopia for present and future generations.

6.1 RELAXED AND ADDED ASSUMPTIONS

Learning occurs in all social forms, yet it is conceived in the emerging information societies as the very base for functioning and evolution. Bits of information underpin and feed technological systems, socio-economic relations and institutions. According to the general living systems theory, the evolution of societies depends primarily upon accumulation and transmission of learned information. These information processes mean not only acquisition of knowledge but the power of organisation as well (see Miller 1978: 42, 854).

The outlined approach is close to the work of Robert U. Ayres and his co-workers who considered the economic system as a kind of information processor. I share the view that produced capital is an embodiment of knowledge and, similarly, natural capital is a stock of information. Some conversion factors are needed for aggregating the information content of different constituents (see Ayres and Martinás 1995).

The models in the previous chapters succeeded in accounting for a number of the stylised facts of cyclical economic growth. However, they ignore the interaction between the economy and the environment. The extended model below includes an environmentally adjusted net domestic product and other environmentally adjusted concepts (see Commission of the European Communities *et al.* 1993). This extension responds effectively to the two major drawbacks of conventional growth models: the neglect of new scarcities of natural resources and the neglect of degradation of environmental quality. The other crucial issue is to be tackled: the presence of feedback from ecology to the economy, in particular through perception of resource scarcity and pollution levels.

We may rewrite (3.10) to obtain an equation for the net domestic product in monetary terms

$$P = C + M + Y, \tag{6.1}$$

where C is the final consumption, $C = wL = uP$, M the net formation of produced fixed capital, $M = \dot{K}$, where K is man-made fixed assets and Y the accumulation of developed natural assets. The stock of environmental assets is not treated explicitly in this chapter.

I have used the assets classification of the US Bureau of Economic Analysis.[2] This classification has an advantage over that used in the Satellite System of Integrated Environmental and Economic Accounting, since it does not describe proved reserves and cultivated land as "non-produced" natural assets when expenditures are required to prove or develop them (cf. Commission of the European Communities *et al.* 1993).

The accumulation of the developed natural assets (Y) includes:

- Additions to their value (in practice, these consist of restoration of the quality and improvements to land, other natural assets and mineral exploration)
- The change in the stock as a result of the transfer of environmental assets to economic uses (net additions to proven reserves of subsoil assets, bringing land and other environmental assets under direct control, responsibility and management of institutional units: for example, the conversion of wild forests to timber tracts or agricultural land)
- Investment for pollution abatement and control to improve the quality and waste disposable capacity of the air and water, or at least to offset the degradation/depletion occurring in the current period[3].

The sum ($\dot{K} + Y$) corresponds to the sum of the net capital accumulation in economic and developed natural assets and the transfer of environmental assets to economic uses. Note that now $\dot{K} + Y = (1 - u)P$. Equation (3.10) is a special case of equation (6.1) for $Y = 0$.

Let $\dot{F}$ be a net accumulation (loss) of the natural capital (F),

$$\dot{F} = Y - Z, \tag{6.2}$$

where Z is the environmental damage, i.e. depletion and degradation of non-produced natural assets (land, soil, landscape, ecosystems) due to economic uses (cf. Commission of the European Communities *et al.* 1993: 510–511). The environmentally adjusted net domestic product (EDP) equals $P - Z$ in this extended model. I am abstracting from entries not related to accumulation (the natural growth of non-cultivated biological resources, catastrophic losses, etc.).

The sum of the value added by labour and of the value taken from nature approximately equals the sum of the value embodied in the consumption and accumulation entries:

$$EDP + Z = P = C + M + Y.$$

The flow variables P, C, M, Y and Z are measured in dollars (or bits) per year, the stock variables K and F are measured in dollars (or bits). Methods of evaluation of their informational content need special elaboration that goes beyond the scope of this chapter. Table 6.1 illustrates quantities for the US economy.

Let X be a desired magnitude of natural capital that corresponds to the carrying capacity of the biosphere. There is usually a gap between the goal and the actual level. As the gap

Table 6.1   The stocks, flows and capital coefficients in the USA, 1987 (trillion US$)

Gross national product (GNP)	4.516
Conventionally measured net national product (NNP)	4.029
Made assets	11.566
Developed natural assets	5.784
Total assets	17.350
Cost of clean environment	0.086
Depletion of natural assets	−0.328
Green NNP = conventionally measured NNP − "cost of clean" − depletion of developed natural assets	4.271
Made assets/green NNP (year)	2.71
Developed natural assets/green NNP (year)	1.35
Total assets/green NNP (year)	4.06

Source: Weitzman and Löfgren (1997) based on the BEA data (Survey of Current Business, 1994, April).

increases, investments in natural capital are increased (corrective action) until the ratio of the desired and the real natural capital nears the indicated quantity. The per capita resource usage is assumed to be a nonlinear function $R(P/N)$ of the net product per capita P/N, the measure of industrial development used in this model.

Exploring the implication of a 3.5-times rise in world output by 2030, the World Bank (1995: 9) acknowledges that "if environmental pollution and degradation were to rise in step with such rise in output, the result would be appalling environmental pollution and damage". There is a perceived need for a 50% reduction in world-wide environmental impact and environmental intensity of 75–93% by 2050 when human populations will likely double and average living standard increase significantly (see WBCSD 1997; Ekins 1993; Weizsäcker, Lovins and Lovins 1997).

It is possible to specify the variables in equation (6.2) for the natural capital in the following particular way, putting aside material delays for simplicity:

$$Z = NR(P/N), \tag{6.3}$$

$$Y = (X - F)/k + zdel, \tag{6.4}$$

$$zdel = DELAY1\,(Z, MT), \tag{6.5}$$

where zdel is an exponential delay of the input, k an adjustment coefficient and MT the monitoring delay.

We have, in fact, added a positive feedback loop to the initial negative feedback loop relating economic activity and depletion of natural resources. A key feature of this assumption is that resource use or pollution has a fixed relationship to output (the linearity of this relationship constitutes a particular case). A candidate is a so-called environmental Kuznets curve (an inverted U-shaped relationship of environmental damage per unit of output with output per capita). A critical appraisal of this curve is given by G. M. Grossman (1995). It is likely that factors that tend to reduce environmental damage per unit of activity can, under appropriate conditions, more than compensate for the negative consequences of the overall growth in scale.

A more advanced approach suggests, first, that there is an opportunity to allocate a part of Y to reduce the amount of natural resources used per unit of output (for example via

investments in R&D in conversion of renewable energy). Second, there is an ability of
the environment to renew itself. Third, this ability can be influenced by society.

The rate of regeneration is given by the function $Q(F, Y)$, satisfying $Q(0, Y) = 0$,
$\partial Q/\partial Y > 0$ (at least for F above a certain minimal level). Then equation (6.2) in a
modified form is written as[4]

$$\dot{F} = Y - Z + Q(F, Y). \tag{6.6}$$

We should modify equation (3.10) to get an equation for accumulation of produced
capital:

$$\dot{K} = (1 - w/a)P - Y = (1 - u)P - Y. \tag{6.7}$$

It is assumed that investments are allocated firstly in natural capital because of the
poor state of the natural environment (for details see below). These investments are
made by the state and private enterprise. The state can use environmental taxes on gross
profit to finance the governmental part of Y. The rate of growth of labour productivity is
also influenced by the rate of change of natural capital per employee. Equation (3.4) is
generalised and presented as

$$\hat{a} = m_1 + m_2 \hat{K/L} + m_5 \hat{F/L}, \quad m_1 \geq 0, 1 \geq m_2 \geq 0, m_5 \geq 0. \tag{6.8}$$

Finally, we may postulate that the rate of growth of capital intensity is not only a
function of the relative wage as in (3.5) but of the environmental damage per unit of
output as well (an application of the principle "pollution prevention pays"):

$$\hat{K/L} = n_1 + n_2 u + n_5(Z/P), \quad n_2 \geq 0, n_5 \geq 0. \tag{6.9}$$

The necessary condition for development is that produced capital does not decline:
$\dot{K} \geq 0$. The debate about the sustainability of economic development has focused on
the degree of substitutability between produced and natural capital. It is accepted that
sustainable economic development implies conservation of at least some environmental
resources. Natural capital is essential to the creation of produced fixed capital. In other
words, it is not feasible to substitute produced fixed capital for natural capital completely.
That is, $\dot{K} > 0$ only if $0 < F$.

I will use a reduced version of the environmentally extended model with equations

$$Z = eP, \quad 0 < e = \text{const} < 1, \tag{6.3a}$$

$$Y = (X - F)/k + Z, \quad k > 0, X > 0, \tag{6.4a}$$

$$f = F/P, \tag{6.10}$$

$$c = X/P. \tag{6.11}$$

The reciprocal of the coefficient of ecological intensity, $1/e$, is called the coefficient of
eco-efficiency in this model. When narrowly defined, eco-efficiency is basically about
producing more value with fewer resources and less waste and pollution (see WBCSD
1997). It is conceived as one of the control parameters in this model. The share of
environmental investments in the NDP, $y = Y/P \geq 0$, is the new auxiliary variable, the
natural capital–output ratios — real, f, and desired, c — are the new state variables of the
extended model based on the equations (3.21)–(3.23).

Let us now derive a compact form of the extended model:

$$\hat{s} = (K\hat{/}P) = (K\hat{/}L) - (P\hat{/}L)$$

$$= n_1 + n_2 u + n_5(Z/P) - (m_1 + m_2 K\hat{/}L + m_5 F\hat{/}L)$$

$$= n_1 + n_2 u + n_5 e - (m_1 + m_2(n_1 + n_2 u + n_5 e) + m_5(\hat{F} - \hat{L}))$$

$$= -m_1 + (1 - m_2)(n_1 + n_2 u + n_5 e) - m_5(\hat{F} - \hat{K} + n_1 + n_2 u + n_5 e)$$

$$= -m_1 + (1 - m_2)(n_1 + n_2 u + n_5 e) - m_5(\hat{f} - \hat{s} + n_1 + n_2 u + n_5 e)$$

$$= -m_1 + (1 - m_2 - m_5)(n_1 + n_2 u + n_5 e) - m_5(\hat{f} - \hat{s}); \tag{6.12}$$

$$\hat{v} = (L\hat{/}N) = \hat{K} - (n_1 + n_2 u + n_5 e) - n$$

$$= \frac{1 - u - y}{s} - (n_1 + n_2 u + n_5 e) - n; \tag{6.13}$$

$$\hat{u} = (w\hat{/}a) = \hat{w} - \hat{a}$$

$$= -g + rv + b(n_1 + n_2 u + n_5 e) - (m_1 + m_2(n_1 + n_2 u + n_5 e) + m_5(\hat{F} - \hat{L}))$$

$$= -g + rv - m_1 + (b - m_2 - m_5)(n_1 + n_2 u + n_5 e) - m_5(\hat{f} - \hat{s}); \tag{6.14}$$

$$\hat{f} = \hat{F} - \hat{P} = \frac{1}{k}\left(\frac{c}{f} - 1\right) - \hat{a} - \hat{L}$$

$$= \frac{1}{k}\left(\frac{c}{f} - 1\right) - (m_1 + m_2(n_1 + n_2 u + n_5 e) + m_5(\hat{F} - \hat{L})) - \hat{L}$$

$$= (1 - m_5)\frac{1}{k}\left(\frac{c}{f} - 1\right) - m_1 - m_2(n_1 + n_2 u + n_5 e) - (1 - m_5)(\hat{v} + n); \tag{6.15}$$

$$\hat{c} = \hat{X} - \hat{P} = d - \hat{K} + \hat{s} = d - \frac{1 - u - y}{s} + \hat{s}. \tag{6.16}$$

Our model is written as a system of the five ordinary nonlinear differential equations (6.17)–(6.21) and the auxiliary equation (6.22) finally:

$$\dot{s} = -\frac{1}{(1 - m_5)}(m_1 + (m_2 + m_5 - 1)(n_1 + n_2 u + n_5 e) + m_5 \hat{f})s \tag{6.17}$$

$$\dot{v} = \left(\frac{1 - u - y}{s} - (n_1 + n_2 u + n_5 e) - n\right)v \tag{6.18}$$

$$\dot{u} = (-g + rv - m_1 + (b - m_2 - m_5)(n_1 + n_2 u + n_5 e) - m_5(\hat{f} - \hat{s}))u \tag{6.19}$$

$$\dot{f} = \left((1 - m_5)\frac{1}{k}\left(\frac{c}{f} - 1\right) - m_1 - m_2(n_1 + n_2 u + n_5 e) - \right.$$

$$\left. (1 - m_5)(\hat{v} + n)\right)f \tag{6.20}$$

$$\dot{c} = \left(d - \frac{1 - u - y}{s} + \hat{s}\right)c \tag{6.21}$$

$$y = (c - f)/k + e \geq 0. \tag{6.22}$$

Valtukh (1991) introduced a taxonomy of societies depending on their information relationships with nature. I present this taxonomy in the language of the system dynamics approach.

$$Type\ I : \dot{K} > 0, \dot{F} > 0,\ or\ Z < Y$$

This type corresponds to a rather strong criterion of sustainable development. Society accumulates produced capital and develops the information wealth of the natural environment. The latter may be imposed by sheer necessity if the society damaged its natural environment earlier.

This pattern of development is a focal point of my modelling in this chapter. The model introduced above can be transformed to mirror the following types as well.

$$Type\ II : (1 - u)P \geq Z > Y\ (hence\ \dot{K} > 0)$$

This society accumulates produced capital; however, its activity brings about a partial destruction of the natural environment. This type of economic development has been dominant until now it is world-wide. In our view, the world's society has exhausted the possibilities of such development that brings about social degradation because of the environmental degradation. Thus this type is not sustainable in the long run throughout the world (see illustrations below).

Perrings defines sustainable development as evolution satisfying the two requirements: $\dot{K} \geq 0$ and $\dot{K} + \dot{F} \geq 0$ for all t (see Perrings 1995). The equations of motion for the produced fixed capital and natural capital are described in his paper by the differential equations

$$\dot{K} = f_1(K, F)$$

$$\dot{F} = f_2(K, F)$$

where f_1 and f_2 are the growth functions.

The necessary condition of development is that produced capital does not decline: $\dot{K} \geq 0$. He assumes additionally:

(i)   There exists a maximal value of natural capital fixed by the biotic potential of the system and the finite supply of abiotic resources, denoted by F_{max}, such that $\dot{F} \geq 0$ only if $F < F_{max}$.

(ii) Natural capital is essential to the creation of produced fixed capital. That is, $\dot{K} > 0$ only if $0 < F < F_{max}$, and $f_1(K, F) = 0$ if $F = 0$. It is not feasible to substitute produced fixed capital for natural capital completely.

From his point of view, development may be strongly sustainable so long as there exist substitutes for natural capital, and investment in those substitutes at least compensates for the loss of the natural capital.

As $\dot{K} + \dot{F} = M + Y - Z \geq 0$, we obtain $(1 - u)P \geq Z$ for all t. Hence type II represents a particular case of the Perrings definition that is therefore the subject of refinement. It is necessary to foster capital accumulation and develop the information wealth of the natural environment that has been damaged on a large scale.

$$Type\ III : Z > (1 - u)P \Leftrightarrow \dot{K} + \dot{F} < 0$$

This is possible even in conditions of a conservative technological base and a small amount of surplus product (the whole pre-capitalist history of humanity) if a society destroys the environmental information. The tendency to develop in such a way would be especially dangerous for societies with fast advancing — up to a certain critical point in time — technologies ($\hat{K} > 0$). It could undermine the natural conditions for the very existence of human beings and life on earth.[5] To avoid it, a transition to type I activity is vitally needed.

6.2   A NON-TRIVIAL EQUILIBRIUM IN THE EXTENDED MODEL

I consider three particular forms of the extended model depending on an assumption about the desired natural capital.

Case 1

Let us start with $X = X_0 = \text{const} > 0$. Then there is no fixed point equilibrium in the model economy. The following s_e, v_e, u_e and y_e serve as an approximation for the respective variables in the long term:

$$s_e = (1 - u_e - e)/(q + n) = (n_1 + n_2 + e(n_5 - n_2) - q)/(n_2(q + n)),$$

$$v_e = (g + m_1 - nm_5 + (m_2 - b)(n_1 + n_2 u_e + en_5))/r = (g + (1 - b)q)/r,$$

$$u_e = (m_1 - nm_5)/(n_2(1 - m_2)) - (n_1 + en_5)/n_2 = (q - n_1 - en_5)/n_2,$$

$$y_e = e,$$

where the new average growth rate of labour productivity $q = (m_1 - nm_5)/(1 - m_2)$. For $nm_5 \geq 0$, $\tilde{w} \geq q$.

E_2 is a particular occurrence of s_e, v_e, u_e, y_e, for $e = 0, m_5 = 0, n_5 = 0, y_e = 0$. So an abundance of natural resources, compared with the scale of production, is the objective precondition for realism of the initial model.

On average, the higher the eco-efficiency ($1/e$), the higher the labour bill share, u_e, in the national income and the lower the capital–output ratio, s_e (for $n_5 > n_2$). Thus, given the ability to innovate rapidly, lessening the environmental intensity makes growth more equitable. The employment ratio is independent of the coefficient of eco-efficiency. This result shows that the policy of reducing this coefficient alone is not sufficient to increase the ratio of employment in the long run. A more sophisticated ecological–economic policy could be elaborated.

Case 2

Suppose now that the rate of growth of a required stock of natural assets is strictly positive:

$$\hat{X} = d, \quad d > 0.$$

It can be shown that if $\hat{K} > \hat{X} = d$ over a long period of time, then the following values are a good approximation for s, v, u, y, in the modified ecological–economic model:

$$s_a = (1 - u_a - e)/(h + n) = (n_1 + n_2 + e(n_5 - n_2) - h)/(n_2(h + n)),$$

$$v_a = (g + m_1 - nm_5 + (m_2 - b)(n_1 + n_2 u_a + en_5))/r = (g + (1 - b)h)/r,$$

$$u_a = (m_1 + (d - n)m_5)/(n_2(1 - m_2)) - (n_1 + en_5)/n_2 = (h - n_1 - en_5)/n_2,$$

$$y_a = e,$$

$$F_a/X_a = 1/(1 + kd),$$

where the growth rate of labour productivity $h = (m_1 + (d - n)m_5)/(1 - m_2)$. Profitability $\hat{K}$ is about $h + n$, while the rate of growth of the natural capital is about d for some $T_{critical} > t \gg t_0$. A sufficiently long period of time is needed to move into a vicinity of s_a, v_a, u_a, y_a. There is no steady state if $\hat{K} > \hat{X} = d > 0$.

For $(d - n)m_5 > 0$, $nm_5 > 0$, $q < \tilde{w} < h$. The developing of natural assets per employee and the reducing of ecological intensity enhance the relative wage, employment ratio and profitability. If the average growth rate of natural capital, d, exceeds an average growth rate of produced capital in the long run, a fixed-point equilibrium does not exist in this extended model.

Case 3

It is simple to demonstrate that $E_a = (s_a, v_a, u_a, f_a, c_a)$ is the fixed point in the extended model for $d > 0$ if and only if the growth rates of produced capital and natural capital are equal at the steady state ($\hat{K}_a = \hat{F}_a = \hat{X}_a = d$). Then this fixed point is defined as

$$s_a = s_0,$$

$$v_a = (g + (1 - b)(d - n))/r,$$

$$u_a = (d - n - n_1 - en_5)/n_2,$$

$$f_a = (1 - u_a - e)/d - s_a$$

$$c_a = f_a(1 + kd),$$

where positive s_0 is determined exogenously. This fixed point is not necessarily stable even in the sense of Liapunov. For this fixed point,

$$y_a = e + df_a.$$

If $m_5 > 0$ and $m_2 + m_5 < 1$, the growth rate of labour productivity, wage rate and capital intensity is $d - n = m_1/(1 - m_2 - m_5) > \tilde{w}$ at this equilibrium. Similarly, $v_a > v_2$. Thus, the economy which cares more about the environment grows faster and has a smaller average rate of unemployment than the economy that cares less. Likewise, if $m_1m_5/[(1 - m_2 - m_5)(1 - m_2)] > en_5$, the relative wage is also greater, on average, than that in the initial model of long waves (i.e. $u_a > u_2$).

For this positive transition, profound changes in the social mode of production have to occur. The necessary requirements world-wide are accelerated, ecologically oriented technological progress, planning in advance of environmental investments and effective implementing of long-range programmes and plans, and international co-operation enabling the developing countries to leapfrog to the highly effective technologies.

The Kaldor stylised facts of economic growth are maintained at the dynamic equilibrium and on average in the long run in the extended model. In the initial and extended models, profitability oscillates around a constant magnitude (d). So the Ricardo–Marx law of the tendency of the rate of profit to fall is not supported by these models.

Parameters used in computer simulations are given in Table 6.2. Numerical exercises illustrate long-term converging fluctuations (*eco-waves*) with a period of about 50 years in the extended model (see the last column in Table 6.2, and Figures 6.1 and 6.2 produced by VENSIM). The equilibrium values are set first for all the variables but $F_0 = 0.8 * F_a$, $y_0 = 0.0804 \neq y_a$.

The requirements for sustainable development are satisfied in the model economy classified as type I in the societal taxonomy. I guess that the view of these eco-waves will inspire the reader's imagination as strongly as the sight of the woman with a guitar emerging from a sleazy cafe in Édouard Manet's picture *The Street Singer* (1862).[6]

The illusive shortcoming of the proposed control is the persistent substantial discrepancy between the levels of the real and desired developed natural assets. The latter is about 2.4 times higher than the former. Still it is not an indication of non-sufficient investment. The real natural capital–output ratio (f) oscillates after the 25th year in the interval (0.65, 0.694) very close to the equilibrium value ($f_a \approx 0.694$) achieving a maximal magnitude of 0.693 in the 46th year. At the end of the arbitrarily chosen 198th year, $f = 0.668$, $c = 1.6$.

A transformation of our model into the system of six differential equations by introducing a combination of proportional and derivative control over the investment in

Table 6.2   Parameters used in the simulation runs

The initial model of long waves		Models of long waves with restrictions on natural resources					
Natural resources are in abundance ("the cowboy economy")		Constant natural capital		Accumulation of natural capital is slower than accumulation of produced capital		Equal equilibrium rates of accumulation of produced and natural capital	
d	–	d	0	d	0.03	d	0.07
e	–	e	0.025	e	0.025	e	0.025
m_1	0.02	m_1	0.02	m_1	0.02	m_1	0.02
m_2	0.5	m_2	0.5	m_2	0.5	m_2	0.5
m_5	0	m_5	0.1	m_5	0.1	m_5	0.1
n_1	0.01	n_1	0.01	n_1	0.01	n_1	0.01
n_2	0.04	n_2	0.04	n_2	0.04	n_2	0.04
n_5	0	n_5	0.14	n_5	0.14	n_5	0.48
n	0.02	n	0.02	n	0.02	n	0.02
r	0.062	r	0.062	r	0.062	r	0.062
b	0.357	b	0.1	b	0.1	b	0.3
g	0.02	g	0.02	g	0.02	g	0.02
s_2	4.17	s_e	7.366	s_a	4.239	s_a	3.235
v_2	0.74	v_e	0.845	v_a	0.932	v_a	0.887
u_2	0.75	u_e	0.563	u_a	0.713	u_a	0.7
y_2	0	y_e	0.025	y_a	0.025	y_a	0.0736
K_0	5.56	K_e	13.083	K_a	5.945	K_a	4.621
P_0	1.25	P_e	1.776	P_a	1.403	P_a	1.428
X_0	–	X_0	2.0	X_a	2.0	X_a	2.378
F_0	–	F_0	2.0	F_a	1.25	F_a	0.991
k	–	k	20	k	20	k	20

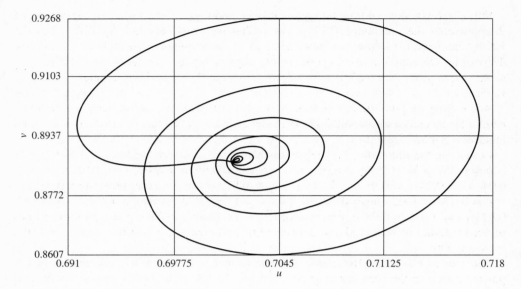

Figure 6.1   The employment ratio (v) versus relative wage (u)

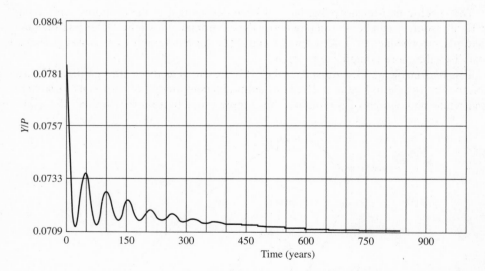

Figure 6.2   The long wave of the rate of investment in developed natural assets (Y/P)

developed natural assets sheds brighter light on this issue. A particular definition is applied hereby:

$$\hat{y} = o_1(h - f) + o_2\hat{f},\ o_1 \geq 0,\ o_2 \leq 0,\ y = Y/P \geq 0.$$

A numerical experiment with $o_1 = 0.02$, $o_2 = -0.02$, other things being unchanged, has shown a new pattern of behaviour of the model variables in the state and state-time spaces. The fit between the real and desired natural capital–output ratios is much better than in the previous case.

Still f overshoots c in the 11th year, it overshoots f_a in the 15th year. The variable f approaches the maximum, 0.774, in the 42nd year and becomes equal to f_a in the 109th year again (as in the 14th year). In most of the subsequent years, both f and c are decreasing, whereby the first is permanently slightly higher than the second. At the end of the 198th year, $f = 0.67$, $c = 0.667$, in particular. This proximity applies to the next years too.

A coupling of proportional and derivative control over the investment in developed natural assets can be also applied in the model economy when the scale effects uncovered in section 5.4 are present.

Let us use the illustrative, vaguely plausible, data:

$b = 0.357$, $g = 0.02$, $m_1 = 0.02$, $m_2 = 0.5$, $m_3 = 0.05$, $n = 0.02$, $n_1 = 0.01$, $n_2 = 0.04$, $n_3 = 0.25$, $r = 0.062$, $v_0 = 0.75 < v_a \approx 0.887$ (as in the experiment in section 5.4); $d = 0.07$, $e = 0.025$, $m_5 = 0.1$, $n_5 = 0.48$, $s_0 = s_a = 3.235$, $u_0 = u_a = 0.7$, $f_0 = 0.555 \approx 0.8 f_a$, $c_0 = f_a$, $y_0 = 0.0804 \neq y_a \approx 0.0736$ (as in Table 6.2 for equal equilibrium rates of accumulation of produced and developed natural capital); $j = 0.56 > 0.5$, $o_1 = 0.03$, $o_2 = -0.006$.

The rate of change of the employment ratio in equation (3.4″) is raised to a higher power, j, than in the previous experiment in section 5.4. Both these experiments demonstrate that stabilisation policy should pay greater attention to this powerful control parameter.

The specific non-linearity that has not been detrimental in the economy with abundant natural resources can be destructive under the environmental strain. Diverging fluctuations take place for values of j between 0.5 and 0.56. An enlarging of the power j above 0.5 stabilises the more complicated system.

This reasonable adjustment shapes the orbit presented as the scatter graph in Figure 6.3 (cf. the limit cycle in Figure 5.22). Is its admirable simplicity not surprising? Like a black and white photograph of a rainbow, this simple projection on the surface of the system

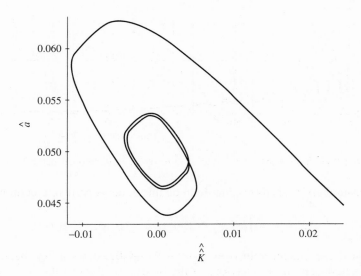

Figure 6.3   The growth of labour productivity ($\hat{a}$) versus the rate of change of profitability ($\hat{\hat{K}}$) in the model with the equation (3.4″). Counter-clockwise motion

behaviour in the seven-dimensional state-time space is devoid of many important structural features which deserve a more profound treatment in future research.

The rate of change of the profit rate is calculated as

$$\hat{\dot{K}} = (1 - y - u)P\hat{/}K = (1 - y - u)\hat{/}s = -\frac{\dot{y} + \dot{u}}{1 - y - u} - \hat{s}.$$

The amplitude of oscillations is smaller but the period (about 75 years) is longer than in the simpler case from section 5.4 (68.5 years). It may not be true for other magnitudes of control parameters.

We have seen that economic-ecological policies produce different results depending on the degree of their sophistication. As George Bernard Shaw once brilliantly remarked, 'to be in Hell is to drift, to be in Heaven is to steer'. The expectation that a higher eco-efficiency in its most general meaning is not compatible with excessively uneven development and escalating social conflicts is supported by experiments in the next section too.

6.3   THE UNSUSTAINABLE PATH

Type III can be a consequence of *type II* in the taxonomy of societies depending on their information relationships with nature. To illustrate this possibility, with the assistance of the above five-dimensional model (6.17)–(6.22), let us now assume that investment in development of natural assets Y equals zero while all the other parameters and equations remain the same.[7] Computer simulations display a resulting decay of the model economy as a consequence of the squandering of natural capital (see Figures 6.4–6.7).

At the very beginning, the investment ratio is 30% of the net domestic product ($1 - u = 0.3$) permitting a fast capital and technological accumulation. Worsening services of the

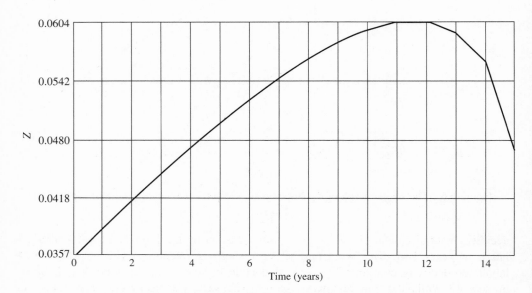

Figure 6.4   The degradation and depletion (Z) of natural capital

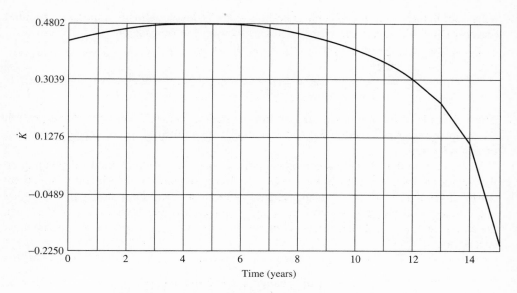

Figure 6.5   The trajectory of investment in produced capital ($\dot{K}$)

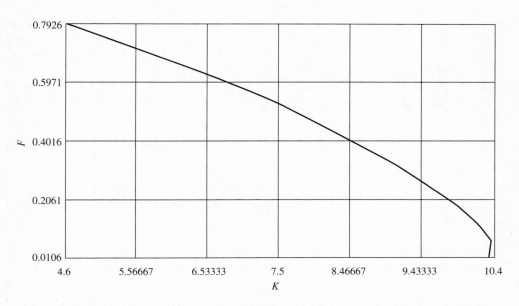

Figure 6.6   The scatter graph of developed natural capital (F) versus produced capital (K)

declining natural capital ($\hat{F} = -e/f < 0$) are masked by the produced capital accumulation in years 1–4. This worsening is surprisingly accelerating. The growth rate of
labour productivity consequently starts to decline in year 5. Its absolute drop happens
in year 13 while the unit real wage grows. The society consumes a part of the net
man-made assets ($\dot{K} < 0$) when the variable u exceeds 1 in year 14. After the 14th

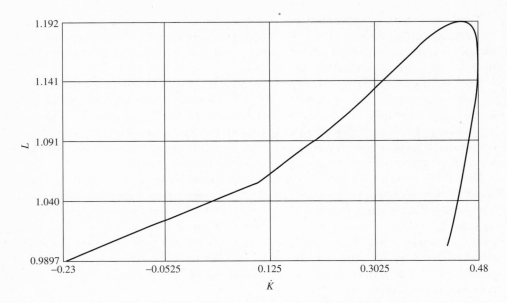

Figure 6.7   The scatter graph of employment (L) versus investment in produced capital ($\dot{K}$)

year, we have $Z > (1 - u)P$, $u > 1$ for $Y = 0$ and $F \approx 0$ (compare Figures 6.4 and 6.5). Declining employment is also a consequence of the unsound form of capital accumulation (Figure 6.7). The economy collapses, thus showing that it is not feasible to substitute produced capital for natural capital completely (Figure 6.6).

The culprit is not the growing labour force *per se* that exceeds an exogenously given carrying capacity and must suffer in the Malthusian fashion, as one can guess. Is it not the social myopia that prohibits usage of the economic potential and upgrading of the carrying capacity? My answer is in the affirmative. Consequently, the neglect of future generations' interests turns out to be very detrimental to present generations as well.

The prejudicial attitude that "the society is too poor to be concerned about ecology" turns out to be "almost" true: the society has not been concerned about ecology and it is therefore poor. A desirable stabilisation of the world's population will never occur at a reasonable level if this behavioural pattern dominates globally.

6.4   THE BEHAVIOURAL MODE OF OVERSHOOTING AND DECLINE IN RUSSIA

The basic scenario based on the well-known World3 model depicts the behavioural mode of overshoot (between years 2000 and 2050) and collapse (between years 2050 and 2100) for population, industrial production per head, pollution, food per head along with the depletion of non-renewable resources (see Meadows *et al.* 1974). Although it is not quite clear whether this scenario will come true globally, Russia provides much evidence in favour of a structurally similar pattern of behaviour. The latter is based on the common archetypal structure "Limits to growth" (but with different ranges of variables compared with the global dynamics).

There are, indeed, several peculiarities of Russian economic development during the last two decades, especially after 1989–90, that closely correspond with those assumed in the Meadows *et al.* basic scenario. Figure 6.8 is a reflection of the ongoing great depression with declining social product and investment.

The German firm Siemens AG by itself is allocating more resources for R&D than the corresponding funding for non-military R&D in Russia's federal budget (see Table 6.3). A growing discrepancy with the world technological frontier negates the labour and other factor-oriented cost advantages and makes output morally obsolete and unsatisfactory for consumers. This imbalance together with other factors brings about, often in a roundabout way, the politico-economic uncertainty and instability in Russia.

Figure 6.9 provides us with a supportive fragmental logical scheme of a primitive accumulation of capital (some important reinforcing/balancing feedbacks and delays are not shown). Two positive feedback loops are very detrimental for the economy fixed on its static competitive advantages at the expense of long-term sustainability. This vicious circle, containing the seeds of its own destruction, has not yet been converted to a virtuous circle of expanded reproduction (the negative influence of declining investment on the production of fuel and raw materials as well as on the competitiveness of the Russian economy is not shown explicitly).

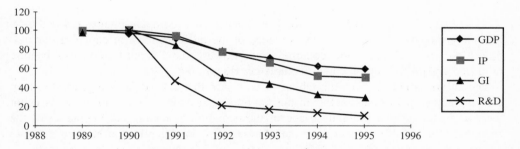

Figure 6.8   Indices of gross domestic product (GDP), industrial production (IP), gross investment (GI), outlays for R&D, 1989 = 100 (for R&D 1990 = 100) *Sources:* Narodnoie khozaistvo RSFSR v 1990 g. Moscow: Goskomstat, 1991, p. 129; Narodnoie khozaistvo Rossiiskoi Federatzii. Moscow: Goskomstat, 1992, p. 14; *Rossiiskaia Gazeta*, 29 February, 1996, p. 3; *The Financial Times*, 13 October, 1993, p. 3

Table 6.3   Outlays for R&D as an entry barrier around new technology

Russia's federal budget	Billion US$ (at the exchange rate $1 = (4500 roubles)	%
Total expenditures	63.3	100
Outlays for non-military R&D	1.7	2.7
Siemens AG	DM billion	
Turnover	90.0	100
Outlays for R&D	7.5	8.3

Sources: Rossiyskaya Gazeta, 10 January, 1996, pp. 3–5, *Kommersant-Daily* No. 38, 7 March, 1996, p. 9.

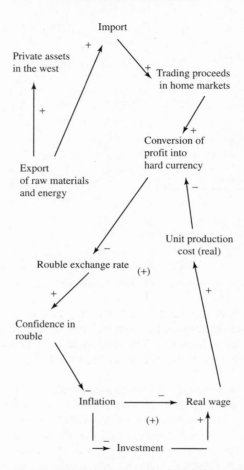

Figure 6.9   Declining investment and (hyper-)inflation[8]

We see again that individual rationality does not automatically imply collective rationality. The contradiction between individual and social interests has developed to a very acute degree. It reminds us of production on a decreasing scale in the anticipative gaming experiments in Chapter 2. The relative and absolute deterioration of the living standards of the majority of the population explains the absence of consensus concerning the content, direction and pace of transformation.

This politico-economic instability, induced by inequality, weakens trust and certainty about property rights, and contributes to flight of capital that enhances instability and inequality further (see Figure 6.10).[9]

Previous papers (Ryzhenkov 1994c, 1995a) have explained the great Russian depression as a period of a deepening contradiction between the transitional social and institutional framework and the potential of the new techno-economic paradigm. This depression has been made worse after the disintegration of the former USSR because of the excessively *laissez-faire* attitude towards science and technology; neglect of the world's experience has also contributed to the inability to keep pace with many other countries.

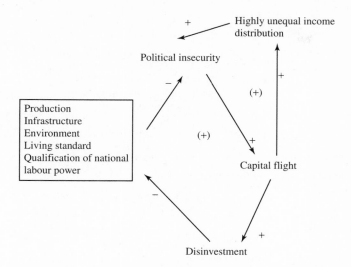

Figure 6.10   Investment and political security spiralling downward

As the technological system of the national economy deteriorates and the stock of potential arable land in Russia diminishes, the marginal cost of land development, measured in
terms of capital and energy, increases. The land yield limit is decreased by a high level
of pollution; it is not restored to its original value because of too low investment in land
maintenance.

While discovered non-renewable resources near depletion, the fraction of capital that
must be allocated to obtaining them increases. The reallocation of capital into extractive industries manifests itself in rising monetary costs of non-renewable resources. New
geological explorations have not compensated for the decreasing volumes of extraction during 1994–99. The evidence gives support to the hypothesis that marketed non-
renewable resources such as metals, minerals and energy are becoming scarcer in Russia
in the economic sense (see Figure 6.11), although it is probably not currently true for the
global economy. This is because potential or actual shortages have not in turn induced
sufficient new geological discoveries, improvements in efficiency, possibilities for substitution, and diffusion of technological innovations.

The side-effects associated with extraction and consumption of non-renewable as well
as renewable resources have become serious ecological concerns. The level of persistent
pollution is already one of the most important factors in the decrease of output and
population.[10]

For a given level of capital stock, an increase in the fraction of capital allocated
to obtaining non-renewable resources implies a drop in industrial output. Technological
regress tends to raise the fraction of capital allocated to obtaining resources even further.
The investment rate has been depressed below the depreciation rate, forcing industrial
capital to decline (net investment in produced capital became negative in the first half of
the 1990s). This behaviour illustrates the effect of the resource crisis on the capital sector.

Type III of the taxonomy of societies may be characteristic of the present great depression. Table 6.4 demonstrates that value taken from nature, represented by potential oil
and gas rent, exceeds total investment. This situation has not been radically improved at
the time of writing.

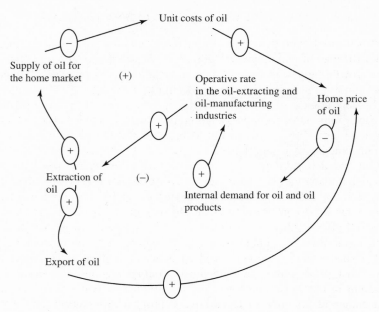

Figure 6.11   The pattern "limits to growth" in Russia's oil industry

Table 6.4   The comparison of potential oil and gas rent
with investments in Russia, 1995

Oil production (million tonnes)	307
Unit oil rent (US$/tonne)	44
Potential oil rent (billion US$)	13.50
Potential gas rent (billion US$)	A quantity of the same order
Total investment in fixed production assets and in developed natural assets (billion US$ 1992, gross)	Near 22

Sources: Ryzhenkov (1997a: 90–91); Valtukh (1996a: 61–62).

I hypothesise that the current unsustainable path is described by a particular occurrence of type III of the societal taxonomy, namely $\dot{K} < 0$, $\dot{F} < 0$.

More precise conclusions are hardly possible if we remain constrained by the assumption of a closed economy. In particular, our mathematical models do not permit us to show explicitly that a great part of value taken from nature is captured by flying capital instead of being privately consumed or invested in the ailing economy. Enhancing resource rent capture by the state and its reinvestment domestically are a crucial political priority, as in many other low- and middle-income countries (see United Nations 1997: 69).

Unlike the basic scenario in Meadows *et al.*, the national industrial system is not producing the maximal amount of possible output at each point in time. This is due to stoppages in production, unused production capacities, a substantial hidden and open unemployment and other macroeconomic imbalances. The amount of possible output also declines through time since there is ample decay of the productive capacities.

6.4 FARE THEE WELL, THE COWBOY ECONOMY!

The present pattern of evolution of Russia's economy is not sustainable in the long term. Evolutionary (instead of pathological) stabilisation in Russia is not compatible with "zero or negative growth" and with the prodigal squandering of resources. The shortcomings of industrial innovation in Russia and the resulting technology gaps in major industries within the broader context of industrial decline represent one of the most serious *political* problems. Since imports of technology are constrained by heavy indebtedness and token amounts of long-term foreign investment, debt relief and revival of domestic investment have taken on fundamental importance.[11]

Changes in social behaviour and institutions in Russia depend upon the transformation of the global economy. Humanity may never experience eco-capitalism if collective learning in pathological forms spreads out internationally. The judgement of the first report to the Club of Rome that significant changes in social institutions and values are needed to avoid global collapse is validated by the experience of humankind.

Persistent instabilities and imbalances of the "cowboy economy" could be overcome with a higher socio-economic order based on better governance and greater algorithmic complexity. This presupposes strengthening anticipatory, proportional and derivative control inherent in the world economy. For the efficient remedy of environmental costs and correct choice of direction of technological progress, market mechanisms should be better used, while elements of positive non-market and para-market social co-operation and co-ordination are to be enhanced.

Renewal is the "pivot of lyricism", the Russian poet Marina Tsvetaeva said (see Hirsch 1999: 23). All things considered, she is right in a far more general sense — it is

Truth unveiled by Time.

NOTES

1. This picture of the French artist Paul Gauguin (1848–1903) is exhibited in the Museum of Fine Arts in Boston. According to a comment accompanying it, the blue idol represents "the Beyond".
2. See *Survey of Current Business*, 1994, 74 (4): 33–49.
3. The extent of externalities in a modern industrial economy was explored by Leipert (1989) in his study for West Germany of "defensive expenditures" to which they give rise (see Leipert 1989).
4. The regeneration rate and time depend on technological factors. There is a perceived social need to direct technological progress to the development of material resources with a shorter regeneration time after the epoch of the increasing aggregate regeneration time of the resource package in use (see Saeed 1994: 124–130).
5. Otherwise an increase in the natural capital ($\dot{F} > 0$) is imaginable (yet hardly practically possible) at the expense of an accelerated destruction of man-made capital. Two roads to the same abyss.
6. This picture is also displayed in the Museum of Fine Arts in Boston.
7. It means in particular that $n_5 = 0.48$. If $n_5 = 0$, their results are alike.
8. Here and below, some negative (balancing) feedback loops and delays are not shown. The symbol "+" means that an increment in a variable at the tail of an arrow enhances a change of another variable at a head of the same arrow. The symbol "−" means that a decrease of a variable at the tail of an arrow enhances a change of another variable at a head of the same arrow.
9. The estimated US$1.5 billion every month long before the financial collapse in August 1998. "The loss comes to about $120 a year a person, or about a fifth of the official wage. As of

April 2, it had depleted the central bank's foreign and gold reserves to a four-year-low of $10.7 billion, about $6.7 billion of which is cash" (*The Wall Street Journal*, 19 April, 1999, p. A19).

10. The death rate exceeds the birth rate for 1993–98. The country's population decreased by 3.7 million human beings in 1992–97. See: *Kommersant-Daily*, 3 December, 1998, No. 226: 1.

11. Foreign debts are estimated to be about US$145 billion (*The Wall Street Journal*, 19 April, 1999, p. A19).

REFERENCES

Allen, R. (1955), "The engineer's approach to economic models", *Economica*, **21** (81–84), 158–168.

Angell, W. D. (1999), "The Fed must fight inflation, not growth," *The Wall Street Journal* 24 June, A22.

Argyris, C. and D. Schön (1978), *Organizational Learning: a Theory of Action Perspective*, Addison-Wesley, London.

Ayres, R. and K. Martinás (1995), "Waste potential entropy: the ultimate ecotoxic?" *Économie Appliquée*, **XLVIII** (2), 95–120.

Baranov, A. and V. Pavlov (1994), "Dynamic input–output model taking account of the investment lag structure", *Structural Change and Economic Dynamics*, **5** (1), 87–98.

Bayer, K. (1983), "Produktivitätswachstum österreichischer Industriebranchen im internationalen Vergleich", *Monatsberichte*, **56** (10), 630–639.

Berger, W. (1970), *Lernprozesse in der Wirtschaftstheorie*, Berlin Verlag, Berlin.

Berry, B. (1991), *Long-wave Rhythms in Economic Development and Political Behaviour*, Johns Hopkins University Press, Baltimore, Md.

Biffl, G. (1994), *Theorie und Empirie des Arbeitsmarktes am Beispiel Österreich*, Springer, Vienna, New York.

Bhaskar, V. and A. Glyn (1995), "Investment and profitability: the evidence from the advanced capitalist countries", in G. Epstein and H. Grintis (eds), *Macroeconomic Policy after the Conservative Era*, Cambridge University Press, Cambridge.

Bowles, S., D. Gordon and Th. Weisskopf (1986), "Power and profits: the social structure of accumulation and profitability of the postwar US economy", *Review of Radical Political Economy*, **8** (1/2), 132–167.

Bowles, S., D. Gordon and Th. Weisskopf (1989), "Business ascendancy and economic impasse: a structural retrospective on Conservative economics, 1979–87", *Journal of Economic Perspectives*, **3** (1), 107–134.

Bruckmann, G. and Fleissner, P. (eds) (1989), *Am Steuerrad der Wirtschaft — Ein ökonometrisch-sozialkybernetisches Modell für Österreich* (Controlling the Economy — A Combined Econometric and Social Cybernetics Model for Austria), Springer-Verlag, Vienna.

Butschek, F. (1985), *Die österreichische Wirtschaft im 20. Jahrhundert*, Österreichisches Institut für Wirtschaftsforschung, Vienna.

Chenery, H. (1961), "Comparative advantage and development policy", *American Economic Review*, **LI** (1), 18–51.

Chiarella, C. (1990), *The Elements of a Nonlinear Theory of Economic Dynamics*, Springer-Verlag, Berlin.

Commission of the European Communities — Eurostat, IMF, OECD, UN, World Bank (1993), *System of National Accounts 1993*, Brussels.

Dosi, G. (1986), *Technical Change and Industrial Transformation*, Macmillan Press, London.

Dosi, G., K. Pavitt and L. Soete (1990), *The Economics of Technical Change and International Trade*, Harvester Wheatsheaf, Hemel Hempstead.

Duménil, G. and D. Lévy (1993), *The Economics of the Profit Rate*, Edward Elgar, Aldershot.

Dunne, T., M.J. Roberts and L. Samuelson (1988), "Pattern on firm entry and exit in US manufacturing industries", *The Rand Journal of Economics*, **19** (4), 495–515.

Economic Report of the President (1988), United States Government Printing Office, Washington.

Economic Report of the President (1999), United States Government Printing Office, Washington.

The Economist Newspaper Limited (1982), *World Business Cycles*, London.

Ehrbar, A. and T. Roth (1993), "Price of progress", *The Wall Street Journal Europe*, 19–20 March, 1, 8.

Einstein, A. and L. Infeld (1938), *The Evolution of Physics*, Simon and Schuster, New York.

Ekins, P. (1993), "'Limits to growth' and 'sustainable development': grappling with ecological realities", *Ecological Economics*, **8**, 269–288.

Feichtinger, G., A. Novak and F. Wirl (1994), "Limit cycles in intertemporal adjustment models", *Journal of Economic Dynamics and Control*, **18**, 353–380.

Fischer, S., R. Dornbusch, and R. Schmalensee (1988), *Economics*, McGraw-Hill, New York.

Forrester, J. W. (1969), *Industrial Dynamics*, MIT Press, Cambridge, Mass.

Forrester, J. W. (1976), *Principles of Systems*, MIT Press, Cambridge, Mass.

Forrester, J. W. (1977), "Growth cycles", *De Economist*, **4**, 525–543.

Forrester, J. (1993). Low productivity: Is it the problem, or merely a symptom? In: Christopher, W. F. and Thor, C. G. (eds.). *Handbook for productivity measurement and improvement* Productivity Press, Portland, pp. 1-6.1–1-6.15.

Freeman, Ch., J. Clark and L. Soete (1982), *Unemployment and Technical Innovation*, Frances Pinter (Publishers), London.

Glombowski, J. and M. Krüger (1984), "Generalisations of Goodwin's growth cycle model", in R. Goodwin, M. Krüger and A. Vercelli (eds) *Nonlinear Models of Fluctuating Growth*, Springer, Berlin, 260–289.

Glyn, A. (1997), "Does aggregate profitability *really* matter?" *Cambridge Journal of Economics*, **21**, 593–619.

Goodwin, R. (1972), "A growth cycle", In C. Feinstein (ed), *Socialism, Capitalism and Economic Growth*, Cambridge University Press, Cambridge, 165–170.

Goodwin, R. (1990), *Chaotic Economic Dynamics*, Oxford University Press, Oxford.

Granberg, A. (1985), *Dynamic Models of a National Economy*, Economika, Moscow (in Russian).

Grossberg, S. (1988), "Nonlinear neural networks: principles, mechanisms and architectures", *Neural Networks*, **1**, 17–61.

Grossman, G. (1995), "Pollution and growth: what do we know?" in I. Goldin and W. L. Winters (eds), *Economics of Sustainable Development*, Cambridge University Press, Cambridge.

Hahn, F. (1983), Neufassung der WIFO-Kapitalstockschätzung für die Industrie und das Gewerbe nach Branchen", *Monatsberichte*, **8** 534–542.

Hahn, F. and I. Schmoranz (1983), "Schätzung des österreichischen Kapitalstock nach Wirtschaftsbereichen", *Monatsberichte*, **1**, 40–52.

Hirsch, E. (1999), *How to Read a Poem and Fall in Love with Poetry*, A Double Take Book, New York.

Hofbauer, J. and K. Sigmund (1988), *The Theory of Evolution and Dynamic Systems: Mathematical Aspects of Selection*, University of Cambridge, Cambridge.

Huizinga, J. (1950), *Homo Ludens*, Routledge & Kegan Paul, Ltd, London.

Institut der deutschen Wirtschaft Köln (1994a), *Internationale Wirtschaftszahlen*, Deutscher Instituts-Verlag GmbH, Cologne.

Institut der deutschen Wirtschaft Köln (1994b), *Zahlen zur wirtschaftlichen Entwicklung der Bundesrepublik Deutschland*, Deutscher Instituts-Verlag GmbH, Cologne.

Institut der deutschen Wirtschaft Köln (1997), *Zahlen zur wirtschaftlichen Entwicklung der Bundesrepublik Deutschland*, Deutscher Instituts-Verlag GmbH, Cologne.

Integrated Economic and Environmental Accounting (1994), *Survey of Current Business*, **74** (4), 33–49.

The International Bank for Reconstruction and Development (World Bank) (1992), *World Development Report 1992*, Oxford University Press, New York.

Iwai, K. (1984), "Schumpeterian dynamics. An evolutionary model of innovation and imitation", *The Journal of Economic Behavior and Organization*, **1** (June), 159–190.

Jeske, J. and H. D. Barbier (eds.) (1993), *So nutzt man den Wirtschaftsteil einer Tageszeitung*, Societäts-Verlag, Frankfurt.

Jones, H. G. (1976), *An Introduction to Modern Theories of Economic Growth*. McGraw-Hill, New York.

Kaldor, N. (1957), "A model of economic growth", *The Economic Journal*, **67**, 591–624.

Kaldor, N. (1959), "Economic growth and the problem of inflation", *Economica*, **XXVI** (104), 287–298.

Kaldor, N. (1965), "Capital accumulation and economic growth", in F. A. Lutz and D. C. Hague (eds), *The Theory of Capital*, Macmillan and St Martin's Press, London, Melbourne, Toronto, New York, 177–222.

Kaldor, N. (1975), "What is wrong with economic theory", *The Quarterly Journal of Economics*, **LXXXIX** (3), 347–357.

Kaldor, N. (1979), "Equilibrium theory and growth theory", in *Economics and Human Welfare*, Academic Press, London, 273–291.

Kaldor, N. and J. Mirrles (1962), "A new model of economic growth", *Review of Economic Studies*, **XXIX**, 174–192.

Kalecki, M. (1939), "The distribution of national income", in *Essays in the Theory of Economic Fluctuations*, Allen and Unwin, 18–29.

Kazantzev, S. (1980), *Macromodelling of an Extended Reproduction*, Nauka Novosibirsk: (in Russian).

Kenworthy, L. (1995), *In Search of National Economic Success*, SAGE Publications, London, New Delhi.

Kleinknecht, A. (1987), "Innovation and profit in the long wave", in T. Vasko(ed.). *The Long-Wave Debate, Proceedings of an IIASA* (International Institute for Applied Systems Analysis) *International Meeting on Long-term Fluctuations in Economic Growth, Their Causes and Consequences*, Weimar, 10–14 June 1985, Springer-Verlag, Berlin and New York, 216–236.

Klinov, V. (1998), "The US economic growth: prospect and retrospect", *The USA: Economics, Politics, Ideology*, **7**, 3–18 (in Russian).

Kondratiev, N. (1990), *Problems of Economic Dynamics*, Economika, Moscow. (in Russian).

Krugman, P. R. and R. Z. Lawrence (1994), "Trade, jobs and wages", *Scientific American*, **270** (4), 22–27.

Kuon, B. (1994), *Two-person Bargaining Experiments with Incomplete Information*, Springer, Berlin.

Leipert, C. (1989), "Social costs of the economic process and national accounts: the example of defensive expenditures", *Journal of Interdisciplinary Economics*, **3** (1), 27–46.

Lipsey, R. (1960), "The relation between unemployment and the rate of change of money wage rates in the United Kingdom, 1862–1957: a further analysis", *Economica*, **XXVII** (105), 1–32.

Lisichkin, V. (1971), *Sectoral Scientific-Technical Forecasting*, Ekonomika, Moscow (in Russian).

Lorenz, H.-W. (1989), *Nonlinear Dynamical Economics and Chaotic Motion*, Springer, Berlin.

Magretta, J. (1997), "An interview with Monsanto's CEO, Robert P. Shapiro. Growth through global sustainability", *Harvard Business Review*, **75** (1), 79–88.

Mansfield, E. (1961), "Technical change and the rate of imitation", *Econometrica*, **19** (4), 741–766.

Martensson, B. (1993), *Gnans: a Program for Stochastic and Deterministic Dynamical Systems. Reference Manual*, Report No. 300. Institut für Dynamische Systeme, University of Bremen.

Marx, K. (1970), *Wages, Price and Profit*, Progress Publishers, Moscow.

Marx, K. (1978a), *Capital*, Vol. I, Progress Publishers, Moscow.

Marx, K. (1978b), *Capital*, Vol. II, Progress Publishers, Moscow.

Marx, K. (1978c), *Capital*, Vol. III, Progress Publishers, Moscow.

Marx, K. (1978d), *The Theories of Surplus Value. Part II* (The fourth volume of *Capital*), Politizdat, Moscow (in Russian).

Mass, N. (1975), *Economic Cycles: An Analysis of Underlying Causes*, Wright-Allen Press, Cambridge, Mass.

Meadows, D. L., W. W. Behrens, D. H. Meadows, P. Milling, R. F. Nail, J. Randers and K. O. Zahn (1974), *Dynamics of Growth in a Finite World*, Wright-Allen Press, Cambridge, Mass.

Menshikov, S. and L. Klimenko (1985), "On long waves in the economy", in G. Blanchi, G. Bruckmann, J. Delbeke and T. Vasko (eds), *Long Wave, Depression and Innovation: Implications for National and Regional Economic Policy*, Collaborative Paper, International Institute for Applied Systems Analysis, Luxemburg.

Menshikov, S. and L. Klimenko (1989), "Long waves in economic structure", in M. D. Matteo, R. M. Goodwin and A. Vercelli (eds), *Technological and Social Change in Long Term Fluctuations*, Springer, Berlin, 145–166.

MERIT (1996), *Annual Report 1995*, MERIT, University of Limburg.

Miller, J. (1978), *Living Systems*, McGraw-Hill, New York.

Milling, P. (1990), "Business systems as control systems", in V. D'Amato and C. Maccheroni, (eds), *Dynamical Analysis of Complex Systems*, Colana scientifica, Milan, 27–34.

Modigliani, F. and G. La Malfa (1998), "Perils of Unemployment", *The Financial Times*, 16 January, 12.

Mosekilde, E., J. Thomsen and J. Sterman (1991), "Nonlinear interactions in the economy", *Dinamica Dei Sistemi*, **5**, 15–42.

Myrtveit, M. (1995), "Feeding your models with real business data", in T. Shimada and Kh. Saeed (eds), *Proceedings System Dynamics '95*, Vol. II, Tokyo, 747–756.

Nelson, R., M. Peck and E. Kalachek (1967), *Technology, Economic Growth and Public Policy*, The Brookings Institution, Washington.

Nelson, R. and S. G. Winter (1982), *An Evolutionary Theory of Economic Change*, The Belknap Press of Harvard University Press, Cambridge, Mass.

Nikaido, H. (1968), *Convex Structures and Economic Theory*, Mathematics in Science and Engineering, Vol. 51, R. Bellman (ed.), Academic Press, New York and London.

OECD (1991), *Technology and Productivity*, OECD, Paris.

OECD (1992), *Technology and the Economy. The Key Relationships*, Paris.

OECD (1993), *Science, Technology and Innovation Policy, Federation of Russia, Evaluation Report*, OECD, Paris.

Okun, A. M. (1962), "Potential GNP: its measurement and significance", in *American Statistical Association, Proceedings of the Business and Economic Statistics Section*, ASA, Washington, 98–103.

Okun, A. M. (1983), "Economics for policymaking", in J. A. Pechman (ed.), *Selected Essays of Arthur M. Okun*, MIT Press, Cambridge, Mass, 145–158.

Österreichisches Statistisches Zentralamt (1981), "Der Index der Industrieproduktion. Der Index der industriellen Produktivität. Revision 1976", *Beiträge zur österreichischen Statistik*, No. 602, Vienna.

Pasinetti, L. (1981), *Structural Change and Economic Growth*, Cambridge University Press, London.

Perrings, C. (1995), "Economic resilience in the sustainability of economic development", *Economie Appliquée*, **XLVIII** (2), 121–142.

Phillips, A. W. (1957), "Stabilisation policy and the time-forms of lagged responses", *Economic Journal*, **67**, 265–277.

Phillips, A. (1958), "The relation between unemployment and the rate of change of money wage rates in the United Kingdom, 1861–1957", *Economica*, **11**, 283–299.

Phillips, A. W. (1962), *Employment, Inflation and Growth: an Inaugural Lecture*, 28 November 1961, Bell, London.

Prowse, M. (1992), "Long wave interference", *The Financial Times*, 26 October, 28.

Pugno, M. (1989), "Labour's share, growth and structural change. The case of US Industrialization", in M. D. Matteo, R. M. Goodwin and A. Vercelli (eds), *Technological and Social Change in Long Term Fluctuations*, Springer, Berlin, 242–257.

Rahmeyer, F. (1991), *Evolutorische Ökonomik, technischer Wandel und sektorales Produktivitätswachstum*, Beitrag No. 52, Institut für Volkswirtschaftslehre, University of Augsburg.

Reich, R. (1991), *The Work of Nations*, Alfred A. Knopf, New York.

Reijnders, J. (1990), *Long Waves in Economic Development*, E. Elgar, Aldershot.

Romer, P. (1989), "Capital accumulation in the theory of long-run growth", in R. Barro (ed), *Modern Business Cycle Theory*, Harvard University Press and Basil Blackwell, Cambridge, Mass, 51–127.

Ryzhenkov, A. (1989), *A Statistical Analysis of the Operation of the Law of Value under Modern Capitalism. An Application to Austria*, WIFO Working Paper 29.

Ryzhenkov, A. (1990), "Teaching experiments with a simulation model of universal commodity production", in D. Andersen, G. Richardson and J. Sterman (eds), *Proceedings of the 1990 International System Dynamics Conference*, The System Dynamics Society, Chestnut Hill, Mass, 948–962.

Ryzhenkov, A. (1991a), "Industrial performance and a market structure (a review of a gaming experiment)", in Kh. Saeed, D. Andersen and J. Machuca (eds), *Proceedings of the 1991 International System Dynamics Conference*, The System Dynamics Society, Asian Institute of Technology, Bangkok, 766–775.

Ryzhenkov, A. (1991b), "Computer-based case studies of capital accumulation and technical change", *Dinamica Dei Sistemi*, **5**, 43–50.

Ryzhenkov, A. (1993a), "An application of system dynamics approach to the modelling of cyclical capitalist reproduction", *Jahrbücher für Nationalökonomie und Statistik*, **211** (5–6), 539–545; *Simulation and Gaming* (JASAG Japan), **3** (1), 86–91.

Ryzhenkov, A. (1993b), "Capital accumulation as an evolving competitive-cooperative system", MERIT Research Memorandum 93-015, MERIT, University of Limburg, Maastricht.

Ryzhenkov, A. (1994a), "Pitfalls of involuntary learning in social bargaining", in R. Hoey (ed), *Aspects of Educational and Training Technology XXVII. Designing for Learning. Effectiveness with Efficiency*, Kogan Page Ltd, London, 59–64.

Ryzhenkov, A. (1994b), "Bargaining delays in a macroeconomic context", in *Exploring the Boundaries*, Conference Proceedings, Organisational Environment, 1994 International System Dynamics Conference, The University of Stirling, 93–100.

Ryzhenkov, A. (1994c), *Politico-economic Premises for an Evolutionary Stabilization and Integration of the Commonwealth of Independent States (CIS)*, Hamburger Beiträge zur Friedensforschung und Sicherheitspolitik, No. 81, Hamburg, IFSH, (Institut für Friedensforschung und Sicherheitspolitik an der Universität Hamburg).

Ryzhenkov, A. (1995a), *Technology Policy for a Future Oriented Social Market Economy in Russia*, Institute for World Economy and International Management, Bremen University.

Ryzhenkov, A. (1995b), "A model of capital accumulation, technological progress and long waves", in T. Shimada and Kh. Saeed (eds), *Proceedings System Dynamics '95*, Vol. II, Tokyo, 813–822.

Ryzhenkov, A. (1997a), *The Problem of Resource Rent in Russia's Economy*, Institute for Economics and Organization of Industrial Production, Novosibirsk, 172 pp. (in Russian).

Ryzhenkov, A. (1997b), "The system dynamics modeling of endogenous cyclical growth", in Yaman Barlas, Vedat G. Diker and Seckin Polat (eds), *System Approach to Learning and Education into the 21st Century: Proceedings of the 15th International Conference on System Dynamics*, 19–22 August, 1997 Istanbul, Turkey, 2 vols, Vol. I, 421–424.

Ryzhenkov, A. (1998a), "Sustainable development under an environmental strain", paper presented at the 7th Colloque de Comptabilite Nationale, Association de Comptabilité Nationale, Paris, 28–30 January, 13 pp.

Ryzhenkov, A. (1998b), *The Puzzle of Unemployment: Retrospecting Kaldor, Lipsey and Phillips on Wage, Employment and Profitability*, Proc. of the 16th International Conference of System Dynamics Society (Canada, July). The System Dynamics Society.

Ryzhenkov, A. (1999), "*An environmental extension of the system dynamics model of long waves*", Working Paper 19, Department of Social Science and Policy Studies at the Worcester Polytechnic Institute.

Saeed, K. (1994), *Development Planning and Policy Design: A System Dynamics Approach*, foreword by Dennis L. Meadows, Ashgate/Avebury Books, Aldershot, England.

Saint-Paul, G. (1996), "Exploring the political economy of labour market institutions", *Economic Policy*, **23**, 263–316.

Salter, W. (1960), *Productivity and Technical Change*, Cambridge University Press, Cambridge.

Samuelson, P. (1967), *Economics—An Introductory Analysis*, 7th edn, McGraw-Hill, New-York.

Schulmeister, St. (1985), "Langfristige Entwicklung und strukturellen Wandel Österreichs in Rahmen der Weltwirtschaft", in *Österreichische Strukturberichterstattung. Kernbericht 1984*, Vol. III, WIFO, Vienna, 1–70.

Schulmeister, St., F. Schebeck and J. Skolka (1986), *Mittelfristige Wirtschaftsperspektiven Österreichs 1985 bis 1990*, WIFO, Vienna.

Šiljak, D. D. (1969), *Nonlinear Systems*. John Wiley and Sons, New York.

Silverberg, G., G. Dosi, and L. Orsenigo (1988), "Innovation, diversity and diffusion: a self-organizing model", *The Economic Journal*, **98** (393), 1032–1054.

Silverberg, G. and D. Lehnert (1992), "Long Waves and 'Evolutionary chaos': in a simple Schumpeterian model of embodied technical change", MERIT's Research Memorandum 92–023, Maastricht.

Skolka, J. (1984), "Input–output anatomy of changes in employment structure in Austria between 1964 and 1976", *Empirica*, **2**, 205–233.

Skolka, J. and P. Mitter (1984), "Labour productivity in Austria between 1964 and 1980", *Empirical Economics*, **9**, 27–49.

Solow, R. M. (1956), "A contribution to the theory of economic growth", *The Quarterly Journal of Economics*, **70**, 65–94.

Solow, R. M. (1990), "Goodwin's growth cycle: reminiscence and rumination", in K. Velupillai (ed.), *Nonlinear and Multisectoral Macrodynamics: Essays in Honour of Richard Goodwin*, The Macmillan Press, London. 31–41.

Solow, R. M. (1994), "Perspectives on growth theory", *The Journal of Economic Perspectives*, **8** (1), 45–54.

Steeb, W.-H. and A. Kunick (1989), *Chaos in Dynamischen Systemen*, Bl-Wiss.-Verl., Mannheim.

Sterman, J. D. (1985), "A behavioral model of the economic long wave", *Journal of Economic Behavior and Organization*, **6**, 17–53.

Sterman, J. (1992), "Long wave decline and the politics of depression", Working Paper D-4329, MIT, Sloan School of Management, System Dynamics Group, Cambridge, Mass.

Thompson, J. M. T. (1987), *Non-linear Dynamics and Chaos*, John Wiley & Sons, Chichester.

United Nations (1997), *Critical Trends. Global Changes and Sustainable Development*, New York.

Valtukh, K. (1987), *Marx's Theory of Commodity and Surplus Value. A Formalized Exposition*, Progress Publishers, Moscow.

Valtukh, K. (1991), "The theory of value and further development of macroeconomic models", in E. Golland and T. Rybakova (eds), *Technological Progress and Economic Development*, Nauka, Novosibirsk, 3–48, (in Russian).

Valtukh, K. (1996a), *The Revival Strategy*, The Institute for Economics and Industrial Engineering, Siberian Branch of the Russian Academy of Sciences, Novosibirsk, (in Russian).

Valtukh, K. (1996b), *The Information Theory of Value*, Nauka, Novosibirsk (in Russian).

Valtukh, K. and F. Pusep (1988), "A teaching simulation model of capitalist production and circulation", in K. Valtukh (ed), *Active Methods of Political Economy Teaching*, Novosibirsk State University, 51–72 (in Russian).

Valtukh, K. and A. Ryzhenkov (1981), "An analysis of personal consumption structure in Austria using a theoretical utility function", *Empirical Economics*, **6**, 11–65.

Van der Ploeg, F. (1983), Predator–prey and neo-classical models of cyclical growth", *Journal of Economics*, **43** (3), 235–256.

Van der Ploeg, F. (1985), "Classical growth cycles", *Metroeconomica*, **XXXVII**, 221–230.

Van der Ploeg, F. (1987), "Growth cycles, induced technical change, and perpetual conflict over the distribution of income", *Journal of Macroeconomics*, **9** (1), 1–12.

Velupillai, K. (1979), "Some stability properties of Goodwin's growth cycle", *Journal of Economics*, **39** (3–4), 245–257.

WBCSD (The World Business Council for Sustainable Development) (1997), *The Sustainable Business Challenge* (http://challenge.bi.no/sbc/sec5/chap.28.htm).

Weisskopf, Th., S. Bowles and D. Gordon (1983), "Hearts and minds: a social model of US productivity growth", *Brookings Papers on Economic Activity*, **2**, 381–450.

Weitzman, M.L. (1985), "Increasing returns and the foundations of unemployment theory: an explanation", *Journal of Post Keynesian Economics*, **7**(3), 403–409.

Weitzman, M. L. and K. G. Löfgren (1997), "On the welfare significance of green accounting as taught by parable", *Journal of Environmental Economics and Management*, **32**, 139–153.

Weizsäcker, E. U. von, A. Lovins and L. H. Lovins (1997), *Factor Four: Doubling Wealth, Halving Resource Use*, Earthscan, London.

Wiggins, S. (1990), *Introduction to Applied Nonlinear Dynamic Systems and Chaos*, Springer, New York.

Wolf, A. (1986), "Quantifying chaos with Lyapunov exponents", in A. V. Holden (ed.), *Chaos*, Manchester University Press, 273–290.

The World Bank (1995), *World Development Report 1995*, Oxford University Press, New York.

Wragg, R. and T. Robertson (1978), *Post-war Trends in Employment, Productivity, Output, Labour Costs and Prices by Industry in the United Kingdom*, Research Paper No. 3, Department of Employment, London.

Zhang, W.-B. (1988), "Limit cycles in van der Ploeg's model of economic growth and conflict over the distribution of income", *Journal of Economics*, **48**(2), 159–173.

INDEX

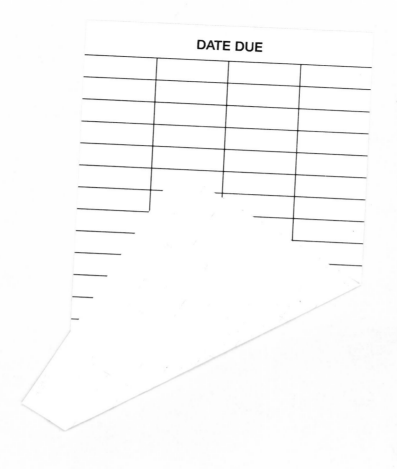

DATE DUE